THE HOUSES
OF HANOVER
& SAXE-COBURG-GOTHA

A ROYAL HISTORY OF ENGLAND

THE HOUSES OF HANOVER
& SAXE-COBURG-GOTHA

BY JOHN CLARKE
AND JASPER RIDLEY

EDITED BY
ANTONIA FRASER

CASSELL&CO

First published in the United Kingdom in 2000 by Cassell & Co

The text of *The Houses of Hanover and Saxe-Coburg-Gotha* is taken from the
single-volume *The Lives of the Kings & Queens of England*, first published in the
United Kingdom in 1975 by Weidenfeld & Nicolson, revised in 1993 and 1998.

A CIP catalogue record for this book is available
from the British Library.

ISBN 0304 35466 x

Jacket images: front © The Bridgeman Art Library, London (fireworks and illuminations
at Whitehall and on the River Thames, 15 May 1749); back © Popperfoto (photograph
of the royal family taken at Osborne House, near Cowes, Isle of Wight).

Endpapers: 'Queen Victoria's Jubilee Garden Party' by Frederick Sargent. *Page 2:* 'Golden
Age of George I' by Sir James Thornhill.

Cassell & Co
Wellington House
125 Strand
London WC2R 0BB

CONTENTS

INTRODUCTION

There is a curious fascination about the dour and strange personality of England's first Hanoverian King. George I was descended from James I via his mother, the lively Electress Sophia, and the twists of fate by which this undistinguished ruler of the German state of Hanover came to ascend the British throne are remarkable. There were at least fifty-seven cousins who had better claim, but in 1714 it was Elector George of Hanover who found himself the representative of the vital Protestant succession.

George I remained German and made no great effort to Anglicise himself. His command of English and appreciation of English culture never rose further than his characteristic remark, 'I hate all boets and bainters', and in thirteen years of reign he only made one provincial tour. But the great literary flowering of the age of Queen Anne continued, as did extraordinary political development, not only in terms of Whigs and Tories but also the significant rise of Sir Robert Walpole.

George's son, George II, was crowned in 1727. He was already forty-four years old and had a solid grasp of English politics. He married Caroline of Anspach who was immensely influential, particularly over Walpole's precarious role as prime minister. George II's son, Frederick, died before his father, so it was George II's grandson who succeeded him.

The sixty-year reign of George III constitutes the longest span of all our kings, only to be beaten by that of his granddaughter, Queen Victoria. He came to the throne in 1760, aged twenty-two, and reigned until his death in 1820. The contrast between the England that George found on his accession and the one he left behind was profound: the period of his reign saw the startling loss of the American colonies and the climactic political impact of the French Revolution. George III lived out the last ten years of his life in total madness, and at the mercy of power-mad royal doctors and his conniving wife and eldest son, who as Prince Regent, was almost as unfilial as Lear's daughters.

The Prince Regent, later George I, had two clashing public faces: the young and gifted 'Florizel' who ruled in the place of his periodically deranged father and who gave his name to the devil-may-care age of the Regency, and the ageing self-indulgent prince whose official marriage to Caroline of Brunswick began as a farce and ended in mockery.

When George's brother, William, succeeded to the throne in 1830, the monarchy was at an almost uniquely low ebb. Seven years later, William's geniality had at least restored it but it was his niece and great successor, Victoria, who brought to the ancient institution the national respect in which it has been held ever since. William also reigned over England during one of the most important, exciting and politically disturbed periods of her history – the years in which the Reform Bill was debated and realised; when Whigs and Tories vied with each other for control in the new kind of Britain that was emerging, and when the role of the King in supporting or negating their policies remained vital.

The monarch who is also a woman must try to reconcile the demands of both roles, and the incredible sixty-four-year reign of Victoria saw the issue illuminated with the most theatrical and absorbing effect. Victoria herself was a supremely feminine creature and, as a loving if tempestuous wife to Albert of Saxe-Coburg-Gotha and the mother of nine children, she found herself reigning over a royal family as well as a conscientious government.

Victoria also happened to come to the throne in time to preside over a momentous period in our history. The extraordinary change over the face of Britain during the industrial Revolution is most effectively illustrated by the phenomenal rise in population, from nine million in 1801 to eighteen million in 1851. The period also saw the crystallisation of Imperial theory and the development of the constitutional properties of Crown and Government. Victoria's relationships with her Prime Ministers varied dramatically, from the beloved Lord Melbourne and, in later years, Disraeli, to the less satisfactory relations with the unquenchable Palmerston and Gladstone.

Her son, Edward VII, came to the throne in 1901 and ruled for only nine years. Yet a warmth of popular feeling surrounds King Edward VII and the Edwardian age. He represented those 'bourgeois kings whose florid forms and rather dubious escapades were all the industrialised world had left of an ancient divinity'. Yet his centrality in the development of the constitutional position of the monarch is crucial. Whilst Queen Victoria interpreted her right to offer advice to her ministers freely, Edward was to pass on a position that was much nearer to that of the purely constitutional monarch that we know and understand today.

THE HOUSE
OF HANOVER
1714–1901

GEORGE I 1714–27
GEORGE II 1727–60
GEORGE III 1760–1820
GEORGE IV 1820–30
WILLIAM IV 1830–37
VICTORIA 1837–1901

Opposite: A photograph of Victoria Queen of Great Britain and Ireland (seated centre) with her family, taken to commemorate her seventy-fifth birthday in 1894. Seated to her right is Emperor William II, and standing immediately behind him is Grand Duke Nicholas II.

THE HOUSE OF HANOVER

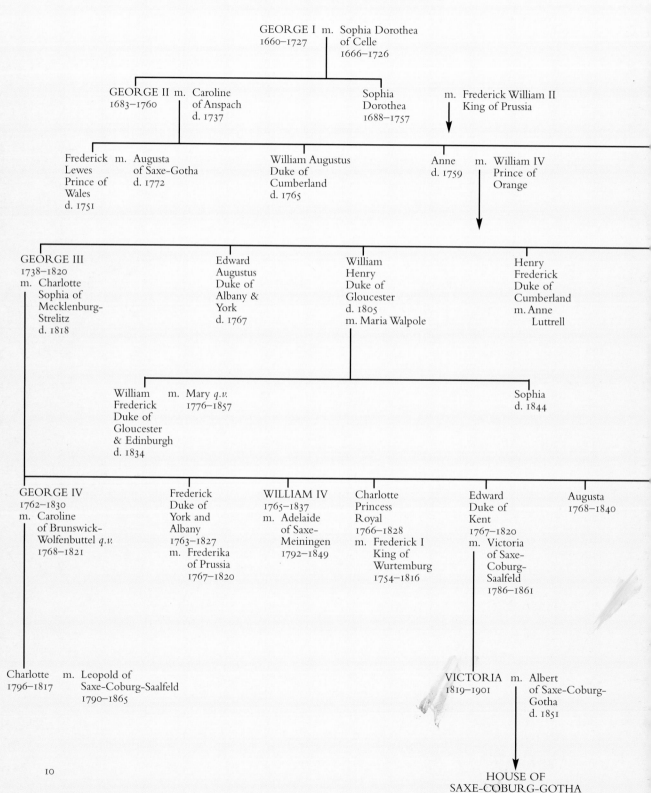

GEORGE I m. Sophia Dorothea
1660–1727   of Celle
1666–1726

GEORGE II m. Caroline
1683–1760   of Anspach
d. 1737

Sophia
Dorothea
1688–1757

m. Frederick William II
King of Prussia

Frederick m. Augusta
Lewes   of Saxe-Gotha
Prince of   d. 1772
Wales
d. 1751

William Augustus
Duke of
Cumberland
d. 1765

Anne   m. William IV
d. 1759   Prince of
Orange

GEORGE III
1738–1820
m. Charlotte
Sophia of
Mecklenburg-
Strelitz
d. 1818

Edward
Augustus
Duke of
Albany &
York
d. 1767

William
Henry
Duke of
Gloucester
d. 1805
m. Maria Walpole

Henry
Frederick
Duke of
Cumberland
m. Anne
Luttrell

William   m. Mary q.v.
Frederick   1776–1857
Duke of
Gloucester
& Edinburgh
d. 1834

Sophia
d. 1844

GEORGE IV
1762–1830
m. Caroline
of Brunswick-
Wolfenbuttel q.v.
1768–1821

Frederick
Duke of
York and
Albany
1763–1827
m. Frederika
of Prussia
1767–1820

WILLIAM IV
1765–1837
m. Adelaide
of Saxe-
Meiningen
1792–1849

Charlotte
Princess
Royal
1766–1828
m. Frederick I
King of
Wurtemburg
1754–1816

Edward
Duke of
Kent
1767–1820
m. Victoria
of Saxe-
Coburg-
Saalfeld
1786–1861

Augusta
1768–1840

Charlotte   m. Leopold of
1796–1817   Saxe-Coburg-Saalfeld
1790–1865

VICTORIA m. Albert
1819–1901   of Saxe-Coburg-
Gotha
d. 1851

HOUSE OF
SAXE-COBURG-GOTHA

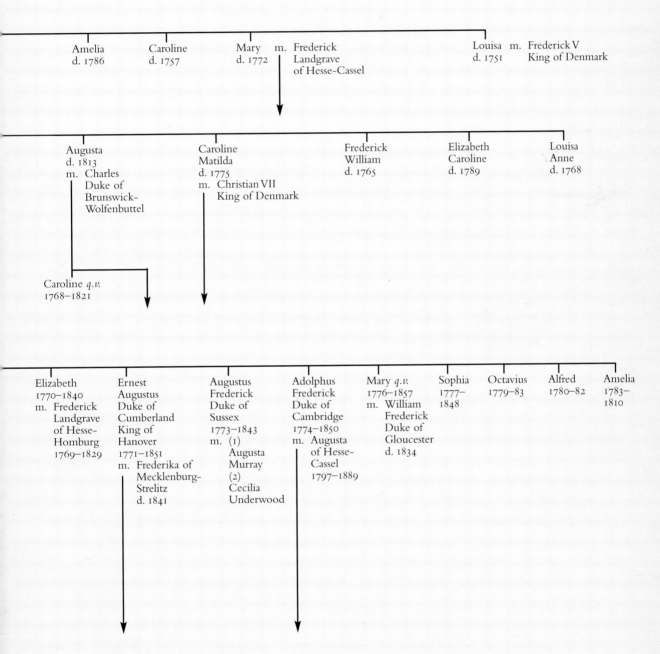

Amelia
d. 1786

Caroline
d. 1757

Mary   m.   Frederick
d. 1772   Landgrave
                    of Hesse-Cassel

Louisa   m.   Frederick V
d. 1751   King of Denmark

Augusta
d. 1813
m. Charles
      Duke of
      Brunswick-
      Wolfenbuttel

Caroline *q.v.*
1768–1821

Caroline
Matilda
d. 1775
m. Christian VII
      King of Denmark

Frederick
William
d. 1765

Elizabeth
Caroline
d. 1789

Louisa
Anne
d. 1768

Elizabeth
1770–1840
m. Frederick
      Landgrave
      of Hesse-
      Homburg
      1769–1829

Ernest
Augustus
Duke of
Cumberland
King of
Hanover
1771–1851
m. Frederika of
      Mecklenburg-
      Strelitz
      d. 1841

Augustus
Frederick
Duke of
Sussex
1773–1843
m. (1)
      Augusta
      Murray
      (2)
      Cecilia
      Underwood

Adolphus
Frederick
Duke of
Cambridge
1774–1850
m. Augusta
      of Hesse-
      Cassel
      1797–1889

Mary *q.v.*
1776–1857
m. William
      Frederick
      Duke of
      Gloucester
      d. 1834

Sophia
1777–
1848

Octavius
1779–83

Alfred
1780–82

Amelia
1783–
1810

GEORGE I *r.* 1714-27

IN 1701 THE ACT OF SETTLEMENT declared that, after Princess Anne, 'the most excellent Princess Sophia, Electress and Dowager Duchess of Hanover, daughter of Elizabeth, late Queen of Bohemia, daughter of James I, shall be next in succession to the Crown'. It was Sophia's son, George Lewis, born in 1660, who became King when Anne died on the morning of 1 August 1714. George had had his agent, Baron von Bothmar, in London since 1710, but it was not until the dying Anne made the Whig Duke of Shrewsbury her chief minister that the Elector could be sure of the Crown. The change of dynasty was surprisingly peaceful – 'not a mouse stirred against him in England, in Ireland or in Scotland'. George took his time in coming to England, stopping for festivities and congratulations at several towns in Holland. It was not until 30 September that the King's barge arrived at the steps at Greenwich. Candles and flares scarcely pierced the swirling fog as courtiers and politicians jostled to ingratiate themselves with their new master.

George was not altogether delighted with his good fortune. He loved the flat north German landscape between the Weser and the Aller; he loved his fine country house, the Herrenhausen, his very own miniature Versailles. George's territory might be small, but his people were obedient and prepared to let him rule as he wished. In Hanover, the Elector decided everything; all expenditure over £13 had to receive his personal sanction whilst the army was regarded as his private property. England, on the other hand, was the most fractious, constitution-ridden country in Europe. George might remember that English ingratitude had often made William III wish that he had stayed in Holland. Like William III, George became King of England for European reasons. The

Opposite: Detail from Sir Godfrey Kneller's portrait of George I, who somewhat reluctantly left his beloved native Germany to take up his succession to the English throne.

new dignity would enormously enhance his prestige amongst the other
Electors of the Holy Roman Empire and England's resources would be
of incalculable help in resisting any power which might seek to destroy
the independence of the German Princes.

The new King was welcomed with ecstatic verses:

Hail mighty George! auspicious smiles they Reign,
Thee long we wish'd. Thee at last we gain.

Opposite: George's beautiful but doomed wife, Sophia Dorothea of Celle. Her indiscreet affair with Count Königsmark, a Swedish officer, led to his disappearance (and rumoured murder) and her own imprisonment for the remaining thirty-two years of her life.

James Thornhill's study for the Painted Hall of George I landing at the steps of Greenwich, after his leisurely eight-week journey from Hanover to become King of England.

The true feeling of the nation was less enthusiastic. Of course, there was a party – well represented in the Church of England, amongst the country gentry and above all in Scotland – which felt that this 'wee, wee German lairdie' had no right to the Crown. George's prospects would have been bleak if the rightful king 'James III' had had the sense to take Henry St John's advice and become a Protestant. In an age when royal power was still enormously strong, the personal abilities of the sovereign were of paramount importance. George may have been an improvement on Anne but no one could pretend that he was a remarkable man. In many ways, the King closely resembled his father, Ernest Augustus. George was of medium height and build with the usual Guelph features of bulbous eyes and fair complexion. His main interests in life appeared to be food, horses and women. England's new King was a shy, suspicious and unimaginative man who said little and at least gave the impression of being a good listener. Certainly there

S. Harding del.

A. Birrell sculp.

Martin Maingaud's portrait
of the three daughters of
King George I.

were good qualities; his bravery was unquestioned and he had fought with great distinction at the siege of Vienna in 1683. Unfortunately, even to an uncensorious age, there was one aspect of George's private life which was discreditable in the extreme.

George's wife, the beautiful but empty-headed Sophia Dorothea of Celle, had soon grown bored with her husband and had become involved with a Swedish Colonel of Dragoons, Philip von Königsmark. On 1 July 1694, Königsmark disappeared and was never seen again; it was rumoured throughout Europe that George had ordered his wife's lover to be hacked to pieces and that his mutilated body had been buried under the floorboards at the Herrenhausen. What really shocked people was George's inhuman treatment of his wife. Sophia Dorothea was divorced, forbidden to see her children again and then imprisoned in the Castle of Ahlden for the rest of her life. Sophia was twenty-eight at the time and was to live for another thirty-two years; perhaps von Königsmark's fate had been kinder.

But what interested people in 1714 was who was going to benefit from the new regime. The extreme Tories under St John had worked for a Jacobite succession and would be lucky to escape impeachment, heavy fines and disgrace. Those who had supported George in and out of season demanded their reward; power and patronage were soon in the hands of a Whig 'junta' of Halifax, Sunderland, Stanhope, Townshend and a rising young man called Robert Walpole. It was not only English friends who expected their reward; George had to consider 'all his German ministers and playfellows, male and female'. Public opinion was easily roused against foreign favourites. The King certainly took a good deal of notice of the loyal Bothmar, of the prime minister of Hanover, Baron von Bernstorff and of William III's old friend, the Huguenot, Jean de Robethon. Robethon was very unpopular – 'a prying, impertinent, venomous creature, for ever crawling in some slimy intrigue'.

As soon as the King had settled down after his coronation, the English took stock of the situation and started to laugh. George just did not know how to behave like a King; the new monarch never dined in state but had his meals served in his apartments – a set of two rooms. In the early days of his reign the King made many *faux pas*. He issued his guards with new uniforms to celebrate his birthday but the soldiers refused to wear their new tunics on the grounds that the cloth was too coarse. With the best will in the world, George expressed interest in the new craze for agricultural improvements. How much would it cost, he

Opposite: 'I am myself alone the charming brute': a cartoon depicting George Frideric Handel who made England his second home after visiting London at the age of twenty-five.

I AM MYSELF ALONE.

THE
Charming BRUTE

The Figure's odd - yet who wou'd think
Within this Tun of Meat and Drink,)
There dwells the soul of soft Desires.
And all that HARMONY inspires!

Can contrast such as this be found?
Upon the Globe's extensive Round;
There can - you Hogshead is his Seat
His sole Devotion is to Eat.

The German composer Handel with his patron King George I in a barge on the River Thames. George's patronage, which was so to enrich English music, began in Hanover where Handel was *Kappellmeister* at the Herrenhausen, George's country home.

asked, to close St James's Park to the public and plant it with turnips? His Secretary of State replied laconically, 'Only three crowns, sire.'

George's shyness made it hard for him to make new friends. He was determined to surround himself with people who had become part of his routine, people who would not make clever jokes about their master behind his back. The result was a very motley court. George's two Turkish servants, Mustapha and Mahomet, were regarded as distinctly odd, but the King's taste for ugly women provoked the greatest ribaldry. One German mistress was very fat and the other German mistress was very thin. The skinny Ehrengard Melusina von Schulenberg, later Duchess of Kendal, was nearing sixty. George's passion for her had cooled but he spent most of his evenings with her, cutting out paper patterns with a pair of scissors. The fat Charlotte Sophia Kelmanns (who may have been George's half-sister) was more vivacious, even though her vast uncorseted bulk terrified Horace Walpole as a little boy. Both women grew rich taking bribes from those who wanted a favour from the King. They certainly made more like this than they would have done from what was regarded as their real profession – 'old, ugly trulls, such as would not find entertainment in the most hospitable hundreds of old Drury'. The Duchess of Kendal was soon christened 'The Maypole' whilst Charlotte Kelmanns became 'Elephant and Castle'.

George's circle was not the most cultivated in Europe. The King's first language was German but he spoke French tolerably well. With his habitual dislike of clever women, he always described his daughter-in-law, Caroline of Anspach, as 'Cette diablesse Madame la Princesse'. Despite Walpole's story that his father had to 'brush up his Latin' in order to communicate with the King, it is not quite correct to say that George knew no English. The King certainly had unorthodox ideas about grammar and pronunciation; on one occasion he declared roundly, 'I hate all boets and bainters.' But if George had none of his mother's linguistic ability or artistic interests, he did have a deep and genuine love of music. George Frideric Handel had been *Kappellmeister* at the Herrenhausen. As soon as his old master became King of England, Handel was able to present concerts at St James's Palace and begin to make his enormous contribution to English music. By the beginning of 1715 then, George was beginning to adjust to his new position, putting down a few tentative roots, finding new reasons to quarrel with his son, acquiring a more presentable English mistress, going to the opera incognito and making up a card-playing circle. Perhaps George was beginning to hope that he could enjoy a quiet life as King of England; any illusions were soon to be destroyed.

George's reign witnessed two major crises – the Jacobite rebellion and the South Sea Bubble. The Jacobite rising began on 6 September 1715 when the Earl of Mar proclaimed 'James III' at Braemar. Although Edinburgh remained loyal, most of the other towns in Scotland welcomed the rebels. From France, Henry St John was directing a superb propaganda campaign against 'the flight of hungry Hanoverian vultures' with their 'cacophonous, outlandish, German names'. Perhaps George should have trembled – there were indeed riots in many English towns – but there is no evidence that the King ever considered packing his bags and returning to his beloved Hanover. The only indication of the King's feelings was in his behaviour after the rebellion had been defeated. Six Scottish noblemen were condemned to death; George attended a ball on the day that Lord Derwentwater and Lord Kenmure were beheaded. It was generally felt that the King's ostentatious gaiety was a slight on the whole order of nobility. George's behaviour to Lady Nithsdale, the wife of another condemned nobleman, provoked even more criticism. When Lady Nithsdale forced her way into the royal apartment to beg for mercy, George simply seized her, threw her on the floor and then walked contemptuously away. George's boorishness soon left him; when he heard the news that Lord Nithsdale had made a dramatic escape from the Tower of London disguised as a woman, he is alleged to have commented, 'It is the best thing that a man in his situation could have done.'

St John's involvement with the Jacobites meant that the Whigs now had a monopoly of power; George seemed almost the prisoner of his government. The King was not a clever man but he was strong willed; he would be no one's puppet. Above all, it was vital for the interests of Hanover that he should retain a free hand in foreign affairs. George had allied himself with Peter the Great of Russia in order to grab some of the pieces of the crumbling Swedish Empire. Peter's success in the Baltic had been so complete that George had become alarmed and was wondering whether the time had come to change his foreign policy. Peace had come to Western Europe in 1713 but the Great Northern Wars were to continue till 1721. It was a very difficult situation and frequently demanded George's presence in Hanover. If British politicians were to serve his purpose, George would have to break up the Whig unity. In the nature of things, British politicians did not care twopence for Hanover, but if there were a number of rival factions in politics, George would be able to invite bids for office. Those who were most solicitous for the welfare of Hanover were likely to get the contract.

No doubt George was helped by the quarrels and ambitions of his leading statesmen but the King's success is a tribute to his personal shrewdness and an indication of the continuing power of the Crown as an institution. George's poor English meant that he rarely attended meetings of his ministers and thus allowed the beginnings of the modern Cabinet. But although day-to-day decisions slipped out of the hands of the monarch, the choice of who was to hold office remained firmly with the King. By July 1716 there were already stories about 'the

Opposite: Sir Joseph Banks, one of the leading figures in the South Sea Company, caricatured by James Gillray. The financial scandal of the South Sea Company in 1720 could have brought down the House of Hanover but for Robert Walpole's skilful handling of the crisis.

The great South Sea Caterpillar, transform'd into a Bath Butterfly.

Description of the New Bath Butterfly. taken from the Philosophical Transactions for 1795. "This Insect first crawl'd into notice from among the Weeds & Mud on the Banks of the South Sea; & being afterwards placed in a Warm Situation by the Royal Society, was changed by the heat of the Sun into its present form — it is noticed & valued solely on account of the beautiful Red which encircles its Body, & the Shining Spot on its Breast; a Distinction which never fails to render Caterpillars valuable. —

Pub.d July 4th 1795, by H. Humphrey N.o 37, New Bond Street

heats and divisions betwixt the King's servants'. With things beginning to boil nicely George could go off to Hanover, so happy 'that he seemed to have forgot the accident that happened to him and his family on 1 August 1714'. With the King's encouragement, Sunderland and Stanhope forced Townshend and Walpole out of the government. The administration was now weaker and was more dependent on George's support. Stanhope was told to stop shilly-shallying; he was ordered to join an alliance with France and Holland which would allow Britain to concentrate on Baltic affairs.

George had to pay a high price for his advantage. In the absence of genuine constitutional disputes, political struggles were bound to become personalised. Bitter hatred between the sovereign and his eldest son seems to have been the norm under the Hanoverians. George Augustus was eleven when his mother was hurried off to spend the rest of her life in prison; the young boy never forgave his father. After 1714 the Prince of Wales made it brutally clear that he could hardly wait for George I to die so that Sophia Dorothea might be released. Walpole and Townshend joined 'The Leicester House Set' which did its best to thwart the King and openly looked forward to the next reign. George I came to see that he had made the wrong choice of ministers; he needed Walpole's political skill but this could be had only on condition of a humiliating 'reconciliation' with the Prince of Wales. The meeting duly took place, apparent amity was restored but, as the Prince departed, the King began to mutter, *'Votre conduite! Votre conduite!'*

A few months later, George again felt his throne trembling beneath him. The South Sea Company had nothing to do with the South Seas. It was a finance company whose shares reached astronomic levels when it received a contract to manage £30 million of the National Debt. The crash came in September 1720, the shares became worthless and thousands were ruined. Highly placed persons at court, including the hated Germans, appeared to be implicated in gross fraud; the small investors were clamouring for blood, anybody's blood. The South Sea crash was a gift for the Jacobites and for a few weeks the future of the dynasty seemed precarious in the extreme. Walpole's achievement in restoring confidence was his greatest service to the House of Hanover. After the deaths of Sunderland and Stanhope, Walpole had no serious rivals; George had no alternative but to make him Chancellor of the Exchequer and First Lord of the Treasury. With complete control over patronage and mastery of the House of Commons, Walpole was indeed the country's first prime minister. A succession of Jacobite plots, notably Bishop Atterbury's conspiracy, were revealed just in time by the prime minister's agents. Like it or not, George I could not get away from the fact that Robert Walpole was indispensable.

In a way, George had been beaten. Walpole's hegemony meant that there could be no question of Hanover's interests taking precedence over those of England. The King recognised what had happened and spent more and more of his time in Germany. George's divorced wife, Sophia Dorothea, died on 3 November 1726; on the day he received the news the King ostentatiously went to a play at the Haymarket Theatre. For seven months poor Sophia Dorothea was denied burial, but eventually in May 1727 George left for Hanover accompanied by 'The Maypole'. A fortune-teller had once told George that he would not survive his wife by a year. The King's sixty-seven years were beginning to tell and, leaving his mistress at Delden, he set out for Hanover full of anxiety. On 10 June 1727, as his coach neared Osnabrück, George suffered a cerebral haemorrhage. He was carried to the castle at Osnabruck and died in the very room in which he had been born. The English had never loved their German King; when news of his death arrived broadsheets declared, 'The Devil has caught him by the throat at last'. The King was out of mind so quickly in England that they even forgot about burying him. No plans were made to bring his body for burial in Westminster Abbey. In the end, George was buried at Osnabrück in Hanover, where his heart had always been.

It is hard to describe George as an attractive man but one should always remember the enormous disadvantages he had to contend with. At least he put his trust in able ministers. The ultimate verdict on George must be favourable; he was very much better than 'James III' would have been.

GEORGE II *r.* 1727-60

KING GEORGE II WAS A TALL AND well-built man, with prominent blue eyes, a ruddy complexion and a nose which was perhaps a shade too large. The new King was interested in history and genealogy; he had a good grounding in the classics and could speak French, Italian and English tolerably well. George Augustus had a very German passion for detail, uniforms, the pleasures of the battlefield and the minutiae of court etiquette. His was not an inquiring mind; in matters of religion he 'jogged on quietly in that which he had been bred without scruples, zeal or inquiry'. Hatred of his father had long dominated the life of George Augustus, Prince of Wales. As a boy he is alleged to have tried to swim the moat surrounding the castle at Ahlden in a vain attempt to see his mother. In Hanover, the Elector had steadfastly refused to entrust his son with even the most minor responsibility and constantly denigrated his considerable achievements at the battle of Oudenarde. Such treatment did nothing to improve George's quick temper; within his own circle he made up for his lack of power by behaviour arrogant in the extreme – 'looking upon all men and women he saw as creatures he might kick or kiss for his diversion'.

In 1714 George Augustus was thirty years old and had been married for eight years to Caroline of Anspach. Caroline, an extremely intelligent and lively woman, was a great asset to her husband. She was large, blonde, blatantly sensual and earthy. A tremendous flirt, Caroline knew precisely what she was doing in charming men to advance her own political influence. George was genuinely attracted to his wife who, despite her artful and somewhat bawdy ways, was probably never unfaithful to her husband. Caroline discreetly dominated George

Opposite: George II's portrait by Robert Edge Pine. During his father's reign, George, Prince of Wales, was given no responsibility or training for his future role and even suspected a practical joke when told that he was King upon his father's death.

SIR ROBERT WALPOLE
DIED 1747.

Sir Robert Walpole, 1st Earl of Orford. Walpole's atitudes were also, for the most part, those of Queen Caroline, George II's influential wife. With her support he held the posts of Chancellor of the Exchequer and First Lord of the Treasury from 1721 until 1741, effectively making him the head of government.

Augustus and was far too intelligent to make a fuss over his occasional lapses with her ladies' maids. She had readily accepted the situation when Henrietta Howard became her husband's chief mistress in 1710; as the Dowager Duchess Sophia pointed out, Mrs Howard would at least improve George's English.

George Augustus and Caroline soon established a rival 'court' where life was much more fun than in the stupefying boredom at St James's. At any rate Caroline was able to provide a veneer of culture; she collected Van Dycks and as a girl she had had a learned conversation with the philosopher Leibniz. The stakes at the card tables were higher than at the King's court and there was even dancing – 'the Princess danced in slippers very well and the Prince better than any'. Above all, the Prince and Princess went out of their way to cultivate the English. Caroline's Ladies of the Bedchamber were all English, although George Augustus was probably rather overdoing it when he declared, 'I have not one drop of blood in my veins dat is not English.' The best jokes against George I tended to come from the Prince's circle; the young Lord Chesterfield told a delighted audience: 'The standard of His Majesty's taste, as exemplified in his mistress, makes all ladies who aspire to his favour, and who are near the suitable age, strain and swell themselves, like the frogs in the fable, to rival the bulk and dignity of the ox. Some succeed, and others – burst.'

But it was not all fun and games. For years the only time when the Prince of Wales met his father was at the christenings of his children; on these occasions there were fearful scenes and after one of them the King ordered that his son should be arrested for threatening to murder the Duke of Newcastle. George I firmly refused to allow the Prince to assume the title of Regent during the King's long absences in Hanover and would only grudgingly permit 'Guardian of the Realm' – with virtually no powers attached. Even in death, George Augustus would not trust his father. The Prince of Wales merely suspected a trick when told that he was now King. When Walpole gave him the news on the evening of 14 June 1727 he is said to have replied, 'Dat is one big lie.'

Unlike his father, George II had gained considerable experience of English politics by the time he came to the throne. The new King was forty-four and was to live for another thirty-three years. He had the time and the opportunity to arrange things to suit himself; most people expected that he would reverse everything his father had done. As Prince of Wales, George had been resentful at Walpole's 'betrayal' in rejoining the government in 1720. Few expected 'Robin' Walpole to survive long.

Unhappy, me amongst the Birds of Prey
Once I'd a comfort, now he's turned to clay.

Opposition Whigs like Pultenay and even the now forgiven St John believed their day had come. George II did indeed ask his friend Sir Spencer Compton to take over the government but Compton only burst into tears and declared that he was not up to the job. Although George had recently described Walpole's favourite brother Horatio as 'a scoundrel and a dirty buffoon', in the end the old gang remained in power. Walpole's triumph should not be seen as the victory of Parliament over the Crown. The prime minister owed his survival to the influence of Queen Caroline. Despite constant rumours of an affair, Caroline found the twenty-stone Walpole physically repulsive, but his tolerant, yet worldly and cynical, outlook coincided precisely with her own. Whilst the opposition courted George's mistresses, Walpole remained on good terms with Caroline. The ministry was safe when the Queen told George that Walpole was the only man who could get large increases in the Civil List through Parliament. Walpole always appreciated Caroline's ultimate hegemony over her husband; he remarked crudely but perceptively, 'I have the right sow by the ear.'

As soon as George I was dead, George Augustus seemed to grow more and more like his father. The court was not very exciting; most of Caroline's bright young friends, 'the Virgin Band', had gone off and married disreputable husbands. The new King's concern for the strictest observance of court etiquette and absolute punctuality was fast becoming a mania. Parties like those before 1720 were now very rare; George had decided that economy should be his watchword. In the long boring evenings at court the King reminisced *ad nauseam* about his exploits at the battle of Oudenarde. To some extent things were enlivened by the malice of the strange Lord Hervey, but Hervey scarcely enjoyed his life at court. 'No mill horse ever went on a more constant track or a more unchanging circle.'

The most striking similarity with the previous reign was the deplorable relationship between the new Prince of Wales and his parents. 'Poor Fred', who was born in Hanover in 1706, did not even look like a Guelph. He had a yellowish complexion and a curved, rather semitic nose. There were stories that he was a changeling but these seem highly improbable. What is certain is that Frederick's father – and even more his mother – hated him from the moment of his birth. George I had wanted his eldest grandson to marry Princess Wilhelmina of Prussia, a match which Frederick appeared to welcome. As soon as George II ascended his throne he broke off the marriage negotiations with the comment, 'I did not think that ingrafting my half-witted coxcomb upon a mad woman would improve the breed'. Later the King exclaimed, 'Our first-born is the greatest ass, the greatest liar, the greatest canaille and the greatest beast in the whole world and we heartily wish he was out of it.' Even George I would not have said that about his son.

In some ways Frederick was rather a foolish young man but he was not really vicious. A little extravagance, a little gallantry with the ladies can hardly justify or even explain this intense hatred. Kings certainly do not like being reminded that they too are mortal and that a successor is waiting in the wings. It is probable, however, that the main reason for George's hostility to his son came from the knowledge that Frederick was bound to be the focus of opposition to the royal government. Even as a young man, it was said of George II: 'Whenever he meets with any opposition to his designs, he thinks the opposers insolent rebels to the will of God.'

The King did his best to reduce Frederick's social influence by keeping his allowance down to £24,000 per annum; as Prince of Wales, George II had received £100,000. Queen Caroline suggested that Frederick was reduced to offering Lord Hervey a half share in his mistress in order to raise cash. In the eighteenth century, however, so long as there was an heir to the throne, there would always be a 'Leicester House Set'. Even with his limited resources, Frederick could patronise the Italian opera of Buononcini and sneer at his parents' loyalty to Handel. George II told Frederick sourly that no persons of quality would demean themselves by setting up 'factions of fiddlers'.

The fashionable world thought otherwise, and disappointed politicians, wits and dramatists began to find the Prince's company far more agreeable than that of his parents. Walpole's power appeared to be crumbling with the introduction of the unpopular Excise Scheme, whilst his policy of non-involvement in European affairs was threatened by the outbreak of the war of the Polish succession. George faced the nightmare that Frederick would use the political influence of the Duchy of Cornwall to eject the present ministers and install his own friends – a group derisively described by Walpole as 'The Patriot Boys'.

For the moment, Walpole survived but his power was weakened; the King was compelled to allow Frederick to marry, a step which would entail a separate establishment and a larger income. The King and Queen chose the seventeen-year-old Princess Augusta of Saxe-Gotha as a suitable bride for their son; the future Princess of Wales arrived at Greenwich clutching her doll. George and his wife immediately added their new daughter-in-law to their list of enemies. Ambassadors were forbidden to call on Augusta; the House of Lords, the armed forces and officers of the court were told that a visit to the Prince of Wales would incur royal displeasure. Primed by Henry St John, Frederick was making the appropriate noises about the Crown being in bondage and exploited by a parasite gang of Whigs. George II had limited his own political freedom because, at the back of his mind, he believed that all Tories were secret Jacobites; his son had no such qualms. Frederick's popularity grew and grew: 'My God,' said the King, 'popularity always makes me sick, but Fretz's popularity makes me vomit.'

Eighteenth-century Princes of Wales usually tried to persuade society that their fathers were simply rather unpleasant and disagreeable old men. George II had said it about his father; now he was subjected to the same treatment. Frederick described the King as 'an obstinate self-indulgent miserly martinet with an insatiable sexual appetite'. This observation was sadly close to the truth. When George was fifty-two he had gone over to Hanover to acquire a new mistress. Madame von Walmoden caught his eye and immediately he wrote to the Queen, 'You must love the Walmoden, for she loves me.' Under Walmoden's influence, the King became more German-orientated, a trait which the English had always deplored in their Hanoverian monarchs. George became increasingly rude to his courtiers; those who had had the honour of having the King's back suddenly turned on them formed themselves into a Rumpsteak Club. Nothing English would suit now: 'I am sick to death of all this foolish stuff and wish with all my heart that the devil may take all your bishops, and the devil take your Minister, and the devil take your Parliament and the devil take the whole island, provided I can get out of it and go to Hanover.'

Perhaps George had reason to be in a bad mood. The same mocking laughter which had made George I so absurd was beginning to attach itself to him. During one of George's foreign tours, a broken-down old horse was turned loose in the streets of London; the animal bore a placard saying: 'Let nobody stop me – I am the King's Hanover equipage going to fetch His Majesty and his whore to England.' When the government tried to reduce the consumption of gin, mobs stormed round the royal coach screaming, 'No Gin! No King!' But there were much more serious blows. Queen Caroline died a lingering and painful death in November 1737. George, who hated illness, was a mixture of irritation and remorse. One moment he asked Caroline how the devil she could expect to sleep when she would not lie still; the next, he was in tears at the prospect of losing his beloved wife. When Caroline died, George was genuinely heartbroken; he had known many woman yet 'I never saw one fit to buckle her shoe'.

Caroline's death had serious political implications. Women certainly had a great power over the King; it had been Caroline who had kept royal influence behind Robert Walpole. Which politician would benefit from the new situation? The Duke of Newcastle suggested that the greatest influence in George's life now was likely to be his favourite daughter; the prime minister would do well to cultivate Princess Caroline. Walpole knew what really influenced the King – 'Will she go to bed with her father? If not, I am for Madame Walmoden, I'll bring her over; Lady Deloraine will do as a stop gap.' Disagreement soon appeared between George and the man who was almost deputy king. Walpole's success was not just a matter of exploiting the greed of his opponents with large doses of 'Doctor King's Golden Soporific'. Not enough funds were available to bribe everybody and some did not care to be bribed. Walpole's policy was one of Whig men and Tory measures; low taxation and peace kept the squires contented. Walpole clung to peace but George II wanted war and a chance to relive the military triumphs of his youth.

The war which broke out on 26 September 1739 – first against Spain and then against France too – delighted the King but it was the beginning of the end for Walpole. It had been the opposition and Prince Frederick which had really wanted war. Walpole resigned on 1 February 1742 but even then Frederick was denied his triumph. George was able

to reconstruct the government by retaining some of the existing ministers and filling the other places with men who claimed to be the Prince's
friends. The trouble with the Reversionary Interest was that no one knew
how long it would take to mature; faced with the temptation of immedi-
ate power many of 'Poor Fred's' erstwhile friends deserted Leicester
House for St James's Palace as fast as their legs could carry them. The for-
tunes of war, too, looked more encouraging. At the age of sixty George
was again on the battlefield. At Dettingen, on 15 June 1743, the King led
a joint army of British, Hanoverians, Hessians, Austrians and Dutch to
victory over the French. George was often under heavy fire. 'Don't tell me
of danger,' he cried, 'I'll be even with them. Now boys! Now for the honour of England! Fire and behave brave, and the French will run.' They did.
Whatever one may say against George II, he was the last British sovereign
to risk his life fighting alongside his soldiers. The King's popularity, at a
low ebb for years, received a tremendous boost.

A portrait of George II's
favourite son, William, Duke
of Cumberland, on his grey
charger. He is pictured at the
scene of the battle of Culloden
in which he vanquished
Bonnie Prince Charlie.

Following pages: The victorious
battle of Dettingen against
France, at which George II
was the last British sovereign
to fight alongside his troops.

33

FRANCFORT

Offenbach

HANAW

Dettingen

igenstadt

french Battery

Gens d'armes

french Battery

Gens d'Armes

B

Battery

2 Bridges of boats

Aschaffenberg

Cronbach

Höchst
Stein-
heim
Seligenstadt
Aschaff
Bobenhausen
Darmstat
Mayn River

N.B. the shaded lines thus — that are
the Allied Army. The unshaded line
colour'd green shew the French Army

A

Hanoverian Battery

the King

D E

The popularity was badly needed when, in the summer of 1745, the Young Pretender, so much more dashing than his father, launched another invasion of Britain. The threat was more serious than in 1715; this time Edinburgh fell, then Carlisle, then Derby. Some of the King's ministers thought they would be lucky to spend the rest of their lives in exile – living in miserable attics in Hanover. George remained calm and the rebellion was defeated by his favourite son, the Duke of Cumberland. War at home and abroad meant increasing taxation which in turn meant increasing the power of Parliament. George might rail against the 'republican' features of the British constitution but he never had the nerve to try to get rid of a government he was not keen on. The events of the mid-1740s consolidated the position of the Duke of Newcastle and his relations, the Pelham family. The Pelhams were to remain in control for the remainder of George II's reign.

The King constantly complained that he was 'in toils' to his nominal servants but in fact ministers still needed royal support. After a protracted royal visit to Hanover, the Duke of Newcastle went to Germany to beg his master to return to England and show his approval of the administration. A modern sovereign would be bound to accept such a request; George II not only refused but 'said a great many things I will not repeat'. There were other consolations; although no woman ever took Caroline's place, the King was fond enough of Madame von Walmoden to make her Lady Yarmouth. George also had the satisfaction of outliving the hated 'Fretz'. 'Poor Fred' had spent his life talking about what he would do when his father expired but it was the son who died first – in March 1751. George put on a show of the sorrowing father but many people did not find the performance convincing; at any rate he adamantly refused to pay his late son's debts.

George did not care for the Pelhams and he liked their occasional ally, William Pitt, even less. George's own miscalculations were partly responsible for getting England involved in the Seven Years' War. England's traditional ally on the Continent was Austria; George had substituted Prussia and seriously underestimated the expansionist plans of his nephew Frederick the Great. George may have been at fault, but Pitt, who had begun his career as a 'Patriot Boy', was the man to lead the country in war. Another round with France was probably inevitable after the inconclusive peace of 1748. The King, 'the good old King' – tactless and short-tempered as ever – took his time before accepting Pitt. He swallowed his pride at the end of 1756 and after that, despite

reverses in Hanover, most things seemed to go right. The year of 1759 saw England's greatest military triumphs – complete command of the sea, conquests in Canada, India and the Caribbean. At seventy-seven the King was beginning to fail, he had always wanted military glory and now it was his. No reign has ended on a grander note.

But somehow George II never quite made greatness; there was about him a hint of the ridiculous which dogged all the Hanoverians. The King's death was mercifully sudden but it was not dignified. For years, George had suffered from constipation; on the morning of 25 October 1760 his exertions to overcome his difficulty were too much for him and brought on a fatal heart attack. Poor King George II died sitting on the lavatory.

English forces assault and capture the Spanish town of Havana in 1762 during the Seven Years War. Britain emerged from the war, the first to be fought on a global scale, as the premier imperial power after largely destroying the overseas empires of France and Spain.

GEORGE III *r.* 1760–1820

GEORGE WILLIAM FREDERICK, eldest son of Frederick, Prince of Wales, and Augusta of Saxe-Gotha, was only twelve when his father died. Even the circumstances of the future George III's birth illustrate the bitterness between George II and 'Poor Fred'. George was born in lodgings in St James's Square because the King had evicted Frederick and Augusta from their apartments in the nearby palace. George's schoolwork was poor, and he was thought young for his years. From earliest childhood, however, he was made conscious of his royal rank. One of his few playmates was the future Lord North, but North's parents told him: 'Bow to the Prince, my son, address him as Your Royal Highness, if you play a game with him, he must win; never, never, raise your hand to him and, who knows, my son, if you play your part well, you may in time get a sinecure post and your father exchange his barony for an earldom.' Under the circumstances, it is astonishing that George had such a pleasant character; he was described as 'silent, modest and easily abashed'.

The main influences in George's life were his rather possessive mother and her close friend, the Earl of Bute. Bute was very much a father figure to George who constantly sought the Earl's approval. In 1759, when it was clear that he would soon be King, George fell in love with Lady Sarah Lennox, a descendant of Charles II and Louise de Kerouaille. The young man wrote to Bute: 'I don't deny having often flattered myself with the hopes that one day or other you would consent to my raising her to the throne.' It was Bute who persuaded George that he must give up the idea of marrying one of his own subjects and should send for accounts of eligible princesses in Germany. Bute and Augusta were largely responsible for George's views on politics. Ideas that the Prince was deliberately

Opposite: George III succeeded to the throne at the age of twenty-two. Unlike his two predecessors, George was born and educated in England and never visited Hanover.

indoctrinated with notions of absolutism can be dismissed – the history dispensed by Bute was impeccably Whiggish – but George was taught that his grandfather was a despicable cipher in the power of corrupt ministers. Bute was a scholarly, cultivated and ambitious man who hoped to follow the example of Cardinal Fleury, Louis xv's tutor who had become first minister of France. George readily supported his friend's plans, but neither appreciated that the Earl's lack of experience in practical politics would be an enormous obstacle to the realisation of this project.

George III was proclaimed King immediately after his grandfather's death. The twenty-two-year-old monarch seemed to have many advantages. Horace Walpole said, 'His person is tall and full of dignity, his countenance florid and obliging.' George inherited the family features of prominent eyes and fair colouring. Although not remarkably handsome, the young King was generally regarded as good-looking in a rather Germanic way. Unlike his two predecessors, George had been born and educated in England. He was entirely English in sympathy, never visited Hanover and was the first sovereign since Queen Anne to speak his subjects' language without a foreign accent. Such things mattered with the xenophobic English.

George might not be outstanding in book learning but he was intensely hard working; he would spare no efforts to do the job of king properly. Few monarchs have been more acutely conscious of their duty to God and to their people. The King was a deeply religious young man; unlike George II's half-hearted formal religion, George III's faith was very real. Throughout his life George spent long hours in private prayer; perhaps this enabled the King to remain calm in moments of crisis – like the terrible Gordon Riots of 1780 – when his ministers completely lost their heads. One of George's first priorities was to clean up the disreputable moral tone of his grandfather's court; within a month of his accession, he had issued a royal proclamation for the encouragement of piety and virtue. It is true that, when nervous, the King tended to speak too fast – a common enough failing – and to fill gaps in his conversation with meaningless patter; it is a gross slander, however, to use this fact to support the contention that the King was already showing signs of mental instability. Compared to George I and George II, George III may seem a little dull and a little priggish. He made his mistakes but, even then, his actions have been subject to greater distortion than those of any other British monarch. The plain fact is that George III was the only Hanoverian who could be called a genuinely decent and good man.

Opposite: Queen Charlotte, who had been Princess Charlotte of Mecklenberg-Strelitz before her marriage to George III, painted by Thomas Gainsborough. She and the king had fifteen children, doing their duty in providing for the succession.

After selecting and marrying an appropriate German princess, Charlotte of Mecklenberg-Strelitz, George III set about destroying the power of the Whig clique which had dominated the government since 1714. George II had indeed chosen his own ministers but he had done so from within the limits of a narrowly defined caste of professional politicians. In refusing to accept this constraint, George was not acting unconstitutionally; he was not planning to establish an enlightened despotism on continental lines but was attempting something no British monarch had done for the last fifty years. Language difficulties, long absences in Hanover and a desire for a quiet life had meant that power had slipped away from the Crown almost imperceptibly. George III was going to stop the rot. The young King eased Pitt out of office, then Newcastle, began peace negotiations with France and installed Bute in power.

Bute was not one of the Whig grandees; he had had Jacobite relations and he came from Scotland, a country still regarded by Englishmen as both foreign and savage. George had a difficult first decade; he had to learn several lessons before he could succeed in politics. He had wanted to abolish corruption, yet in order to keep Bute in power he had to resort to the very tactics he deplored in others. Sadly he concluded, 'We must call in bad men to govern bad men.' Bute managed to get the peace with France through Parliament and then resigned rather than face an all-out attack. Prime ministers followed in rapid succession – George Grenville, Lord Rockingham, William Pitt and the Duke of Grafton. Ministers claimed that political instability was caused by George's failure to give his official advisers proper support; ignoring his constitutional duty to consult them in all things, he 'went behind the curtain' to seek advice from Bute. Grenville had some cause for complaint but, instead of trying to win the King's confidence, he indulged in long lectures upbraiding George for ingratitude. The King declared, 'When he has wearied me for two hours, he looks at his watch to see if he may not tire me for an hour more.' All the time, George was subjected to crude abuse from the gutter press, whilst the irresponsible libertine John Wilkes stirred the London mob to riot and sedition.

George had shown that governments which did not enjoy the monarch's full confidence tended to have a short life but, equally, prime ministers could stay in office only if they had the respect and votes of Parliament. Patronage might help but it was not enough on its own; was there anyone in politics who was genuinely acceptable to both King and Parliament? In 1770 George thought he had found his man – Lord Frederick North, 'the man who lost America' and allegedly the worst prime minister in British history. George's selection of North seems proof of the King's stupidity – 'a fool chosen by a fool'. Yet one cannot so dismiss a man who retained a working majority in Parliament for ten years. Within the context of British politics George's judgement was sound. The 'green boy' of 1760 had become a shrewd politician; North was a good Parliament man, an able speaker and would have been an excellent peacetime premier. Claims that George wanted to enslave his colonial subjects are absurd. The King certainly supported his prime minister's attempts to suppress the American rebels; perhaps George III might have shown more imagination but then the same charge can be made against almost all of the political establishment. Those who became advocates of American Independence were converted only very late in the day when the war was virtually lost and generally perceived to be so. Kings are expected to be consistent.

AFFABILITY.

"Well, Friend, where a'you going, Hay? __ whats your Name, hay? __ where d'ye Live, hay? __ hay?"

The King was very interested in farming and agricultural improvement, and showed a level of enthusiasm for rural matters here lampooned in a contemporary satirical illustration. He was also inclined to add 'hey, hey' to the end of sentences.

The loss of America was a terrible blow. Catherine the Great of Russia said, 'Rather than have granted America her Independence as my brother monarch, King George, has done, I would have fired a pistol at my own head.' The political problems created by the collapse of North's ministry were enormous. Charles James Fox described the King as an arbitrary despot who had squandered his subjects' blood and treasure in his mad lust for revenge. After North, Lord Rockingham took office with a programme of reducing royal influence in politics, but even this was not enough. The country was soon confronted with the astonishing spectacle of Fox joining up with the now discredited North to impose even greater restrictions and humiliations. 'The King's closet had been

The King and Napleon playing chess, showing Napoleon's early flair in the eponymous wars. However, George's choice of Pitt the Younger was crucial in securing Napoleon's and Revolutionary France's eventual defeat.

stormed' by men George had reason to hate. It must have seemed absurd to suggest that anyone short of a political genius could ever recapture for the King the right of choosing his own ministers. To the astonishment of everyone, this is what George proceeded to do.

On 18 December 1783 the House of Lords rejected the government's East India Bill – at 1 a.m. the King sent out notices of dismissal to all members of the Fox–North coalition. George had chosen his moment carefully; the country would not permit an illegitimate extension of royal power or of ministerial power against the Crown. Influential people felt that Fox was going too far and swung around to support the King. The next prime minister, William Pitt the Younger, was only twenty-four. Pitt was very much George's personal choice; for several months the new government was constantly defeated in

Parliament, yet the King refused to think of accepting its resignation. When Pitt felt that the time had come for a general election, George put all the resources of the Crown behind his protégé. The result was a tremendous defeat for Fox. The King's choice of Pitt is probably the best proof of royal sagacity. Pitt was to remain in power for twenty-one years and was to lead England in the terrible struggle with Revolutionary France. In such perilous times it was better that Pitt, rather than the wild Charles James Fox, should be running the country.

The mid-1780s were probably the best years of George's reign. Under Pitt's guidance, Britain was fast recovering her prosperity and self-confidence. George III was in vigorous middle age, his figure kept trim and youthful by a spartan diet and plenty of exercise. Apart from one illness in 1765 the King had enjoyed excellent health throughout his reign. George was a good and faithful husband; although not the most exciting of women, Queen Charlotte was at least contented with her lot. She declared that since her marriage she had never known a real moment of sorrow. There had been no less than fifteen children to the marriage; no one could say that George had not secured the succession. The atmosphere at court was more relaxed. The King was less prudish than in the early years of the reign and laughed heartily at Cibber's play *She Would and She Would Not*. Absence of political pressure meant that George was able to develop his knowledge of botany and write pamphlets on agricultural improvements under the pen name of Ralph Robinson. Intellectually the King had been a slow starter but he had caught up; in the 1780s he compared favourably with most European monarchs, certainly with Louis XVI.

The one black spot was the growing antagonism between George III and his eldest son, the future Prince Regent. The same conflicts which had soured the relationship between George I and George Augustus and between George II and 'Poor Fred' were appearing yet again. There were faults on both sides; George III's great failing was that he was over-protective. He genuinely loved his son but he wanted the Prince of Wales to remain a child for ever. The 'cotton wool' atmosphere of Kew Palace was far too restrictive for the high-spirited young Prince and the desire to rebel against it led him into all kinds of wickedness. But the King's reaction to his son's follies was more of sorrow than anger; the Prince of Wales really had far less to complain about than 'Poor Fred' had done.

Such was the state of the country and the royal family when George III 'went mad'. The King had not been well in the summer of 1788; he had an alarming attack of convulsions after riding in the rain on 16 October. George's manner was thought odd and he seemed never to stop talking. It was about this time that the famous Oak Tree incident is alleged to have occurred with the King talking to a tree as if it were the King of Prussia. This story was put about by a page who had been dismissed from the royal service so its veracity must be questionable. On 5 November 1788, however, there were obvious signs of derangement. At dinner in Windsor Castle the King attacked the Prince of Wales and tried to smash his head against the wall. George was talking non-stop gibberish, foam was coming from his mouth and his eyes were so bloodshot that they looked like currant jelly.

When it was clear that the King would survive although he might never recover his reason, he was removed from Windsor and taken to Kew. George's doctors may have thought they were doing the right thing, but there can be no doubt that their treatment was abominably cruel and only served to delay the patient's recovery. George's chief doctor at Kew was Dr Francis Willis, the proprietor of a private lunatic asylum in Lincoln. Lectures, threats and the strait-jacket played a large part in Willis's treatment. If the King refused food or was restless, his legs were tied to the bed and a band strapped across his chest. Later, Willis introduced a special iron chair to restrain his patient; with bitter irony George called this terrible contraption his 'coronation chair'. As the real thing had brought him respect and honour so this travesty brought only humiliation. Willis was not the only tormentor; Dr Warren insisted on putting poultices of Spanish fly and mustard all over the King's body; the idea was that the painful blisters which resulted would draw out the 'evil humours'. Despite the efforts of his doctors, George III gradually regained his reason and was well enough to attend a service of thanksgiving for his recovery in St Paul's Cathedral on 23 April 1789.

Ever since that time, doctors and historians have argued about the nature of George III's madness. One school believes that the King's illness is best explained in psychological terms, the other thinks that George was suffering from a rare physical illness. If the second explanation is correct then, in the strict sense, George III was never 'mad' at all. It has been variously claimed that George III had an Oedipus complex about his mother, that he suffered from sexual repression by remaining faithful to an ugly queen, or even that he was burdened with the guilt of a secret marriage in 1757 to 'the Fair Quakeress' Hannah Lightfoot. Others believe that the strains of kingship were too much for

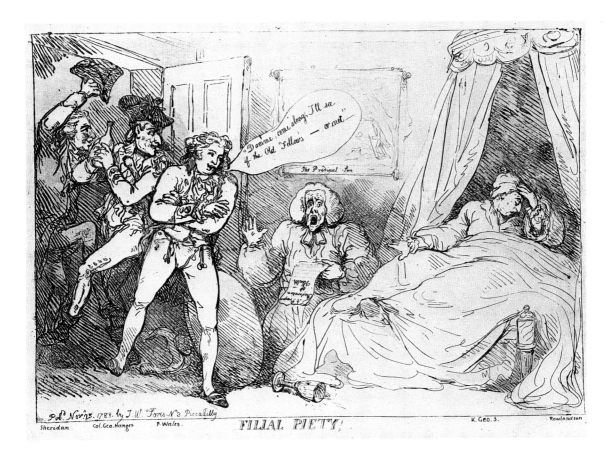

Pub.d Nov.25. 1788. by J.W. Fores N.o 3 Piccadilly

Sheridan   Col.Geo.Hanger   P.Wales.   *FILIAL PIETY!*   K. Geo. 3.   Rowlandson

George and see the traumatic loss of America as the crucial factor. George III, it seems, might have been an excellent country squire but he was just not up to being King. More recently, attention has been focused on the physical symptoms which accompanied George's illness – rapid pulse, an angry rash, yellow or bloodshot eyes, swollen feet and red-coloured urine. From this, it is possible to argue that George III was suffering from porphyria, an unusual disease which was not properly understood until the 1930s. Porphyria is the name given to a distu bance of the porphyrin metabolism, the process which creates red pigment in the blood. If too much of this pigment is produced, the urine becomes discoloured and the whole nervous system, including the brain, is poisoned. The porphyria explanation may sound too exotic but it does fit the known facts very well. Above all, it has the advantage of demolishing theories that George III was rather unbalanced throughout his life.

An engraving published in November 1788 showing the Prince of Wales and some of his drinking friends, including the author Sheridan, bursting in upon George III. This cartoon was published at the time that the king's health had become a matter for serious concern.

George's illness showed how much the people of his country loved and respected him. In November 1788 there was panic on the Stock Exchange when it was thought that the King would die and be succeeded by the Prince of Wales. Most people were delighted that George recovered in time to prevent the implementation of the provisions of the Regency Bill. The royal tour of the south of England in the summer of 1789 was a tremendous success, crowds and triumphal arches in every village and a local band wading into the sea to play 'God Save the King' when George went bathing at Weymouth.

George III was less outraged by the French Revolution than some European monarchs. He felt that it was divine punishment of the House of Bourbon for its unnatural support of the rebels in the Thirteen Colonies (in America). Of course, the outbreak of the war with France in 1793 brought serious strains and republican ideas were formed in some circles. The King was the object of a number of assassination attempts. On 15 May 1800 George was standing in the royal box of the Drury Lane Theatre when a man in the pit stood on a box and fired two pistol shots at the King. The bullets missed by inches and embedded themselves in the panelling of the box. George ordered the performance to continue and was so calm that he went to sleep in the interval.

The King had two brief relapses into his old complaint in 1801 and 1804 but it is far from true that the King was unimportant by the first decade of the new century. George's main concern now was to prevent the passage of 'Catholic Emancipation', a measure which would allow Roman Catholics to sit in Parliament. The King believed that if he agreed to such a measure he would be guilty of breaking the solemn coronation oath to defend the Protestant religion. Such a view may seem incredibly benighted but it was certainly the opinion of the vast majority of George's subjects. In his determination to stop Catholic Emancipation George forced Pitt out of office in 1801 and summarily ejected the Grenville ministry in 1807. To the end of his active life, therefore, the King maintained the vital principle that the choice of ministers remained with the Crown.

Until he was over seventy, George III had been 'mad' for less than six months. It was only in 1810 that permanent insanity descended upon him. The last decade of George's life was very sad. He was a blind old man with a long white beard, wearing a violet dressing gown and shambling around an isolated set of rooms in Windsor Castle. Only the Star of the Order of the Garter which he kept pinned to his chest was

a reminder that this wreck of a man was King of England. George found release on 29 January 1820; he was nearly eighty-two. The Lear-like figure of the last years was still revered by his people. They knew that 'Farmer George' had been a good man and a good king. Many books have been written to explain why the monarchy fell in France and survived in England; historians would do well to consider whether the personal integrity of King George III did not have a lot to do with it.

George III bathing – to the strains of *God Save the King* – at his favourite holiday resort, Weymouth, in 1789. The royal tour of the south of England followed George's recently recovery from his first period of major illness.

49

GEORGE IV *r.* 1820-30

GEORGE IV WAS KING FOR ONLY ten years, from 1820 to 1830, but, as Prince Regent from 1812 to 1820, he exercised all the powers of sovereign for a total of eighteen years. There can be no doubt that George wasted his great gifts and abilities. As a young man the Prince was outstandingly handsome and charming. He was tall and dignified in his bearing and Mrs 'Perdita' Robinson was only one of the many women who found it impossible to forget 'the grace of his person, the irresistible sweetness of his smile, the tenderness of his melodious yet manly voice'. A taste for gargantuan meals and heavy drinking soon changed that. By the time he had reached his late thirties, George had become very like the repellent creature depicted in Gillray's cartoon 'A Voluptuary under the horrors of Digestion'. This shows George recovering from an enormous meal at Carlton House, his huge belly bursting from his breeches and his florid face on the verge of apoplexy. He is surrounded by empty wine bottles, unpaid bills for which an overflowing chamber-pot acts as paperweight, and various patent medicines including famous cures for venereal disease. There is certainly some justification for Leigh Hunt's damning comments on George's fiftieth birthday in 1812: 'A libertine over head and ears in debt and disgrace, a despiser of domestic ties, the companion of demi-reps, a man who has just closed half a century without a single claim on the gratitude of his country or the respect of posterity.'

More than anyone else, the Prince was responsible for the cruel slander that George III spent most of his life insane. When George III was desperately ill in November 1788, his eldest son was going round the London clubs giving intimate details of the King's condition, mimicking

Opposite: A portrait of George IV by Sir Thomas Laurence. Unlike his philistine Hanoverian predecessors, George had a distinct personal style and taste that found expression in the palaces he built, particularly the fabulous Brighton Pavilion.

A

BILL

To deprive Her MAJESTY Caroline Amelia Elizabeth of the Title, Prerogatives, Rights, Privileges, and Pretensions of Queen Consort of this Realm, and to dissolve the Marriage between His MAJESTY and the said Queen.

Note.—*The first column contains a Copy of the Bill—The second column contains the* CLAUSES THAT DROPT OUT, *and which are now proposed to be* restored.

WHEREAS in the year one thousand eight hundred and fourteen, Her MAJESTY, *Caroline Amelia Elizabeth,* then Princess of *Wales,* and now Queen Consort of this Realm, being at *Milan,* in *Italy,* engaged in her service in a menial situation, one *Bartolomo Pergami,* otherwise *Bartolomo Bergami,* a foreigner of low station, who had before served in a similar capacity:

AND WHEREAS, after the said *Bartolomo Pergami,* otherwise *Bartolomo Bergami,* had so entered the service of her Royal Highness the said Princess of *Wales,* a most unbecoming and degrading intimacy commenced between Her Royal Highness and the said *Bartolomo Pergami,* otherwise *Bartolomo Bergami:*

AND WHEREAS her Royal Highness not only advanced the said *Bartolomo Pergami,* otherwise *Bartolomo Bergami,* to a high situation in her Royal Highness's household, and received into her service many of his near relations, some of them in

WHEREAS on the eighth day of *April,* one thousand seven hundred and ninety-five, your MAJESTY, then being Prince of *Wales* and Heir apparent to the throne of these Realms, intermarried with the Princess *Caroline Amelia Elizabeth* of *Brunswick,* by whom, on the seventh day of *January,* one thousand seven hundred and ninety-six, you had issue the late Princess *Charlotte* of happy memory.

AND WHEREAS on the thirtieth day of *April,* in the said year one thousand seven hundred and ninety-six, your MAJESTY was graciously pleased to write to Her said Majesty, in and by a letter of that date, as follows ;—" *Our inclinations* " *are not in our power, nor should* " *either of us be held answerable to* " *the other* ; because nature has not " *made us suitable to each other* ;" and in which said letter your Majesty defined to Her Majesty, the terms whereon you proposed from thenceforth to live wholly and entirely

The Bill George tried to force through Parliament to dissolve his empty marriage to Queen Caroline and deny her right to a title.

his ravings and even speculating on a *coup d'état* to take over full royal power. The Prince's behaviour to women was no better. His affair with Perdita Robinson ended with a curt note saying that they must meet no more. In 1784, after a brief affair with Lady Melbourne – who exploited her position to get for her husband the appropriate job of Gentleman of the Bedchamber – George met a rather strait-laced Roman Catholic widow. Maria Fitzherbert was five years older than the Prince; although attracted to the young man, she resolutely refused to become his mistress. In the end, the only way to overcome her scruples was to go through a form of marriage. The Reverend Robert Butt, then confined to the debtors' prison, agreed to perform the ceremony on condition that he was given a bishopric when George became King. Although canonically valid, the marriage was null and void from the beginning under the terms of the 1772 Royal Marriages Act and was to prove a great embarrassment for George's Whig friends who tried to deny its existence in Parliament.

George was genuinely in love with Mrs Fitzherbert – for a while – but it was not long before he left her for Lady Jersey, who was already a grandmother. George's extravagance frequently got him into difficulties; as early as 1783, George III denounced plans to increase his son's allowance as 'a shameful squandering of public money to gratify the passions of an ill-advised young man'. But George's greatest disaster came in 1795 when he agreed to marry his cousin, Caroline of Brunswick, in order to persuade Parliament to write off his debts. George was appalled when he met his bride to be; his first words were 'I am not well, pray get me a glass of brandy'. In turn, Caroline found George 'very stout and by no means as handsome as his portrait'. The Prince was helplessly drunk at the wedding.

Caroline was scarcely an ideal Princess of Wales; she was fat, coarse, vulgar and unwashed. After the birth of a daughter, Princess Charlotte, on 7 January 1796, the couple lived apart. In ten years, Caroline spent much of her time in Italy and, according to her accusers, lived 'in a most unbecoming and disgusting intimacy' with Bartolomo Pergami, the handsome Chamberlain of the Queen's Household. In 1820 Caroline returned to England to claim her rights as Queen and quickly became a focus of popular discontent against George and his government. Slogans appeared all over London – 'The Queen for ever! The King in the River!' George forced the government to bring in a Bill which deprived 'Her Majesty Caroline Amelia Elizabeth of the title of Queen' and declared her marriage to the King 'for ever wholly dissolved, annulled and made void'. A great deal of titillating but not altogether trustworthy evidence was produced and the Bill was eventually dropped. Caroline appeared at George's coronation only to be turned away from the doors of Westminster Abbey. Fortunately for the King's peace of mind, his unsuitable Queen died suddenly on 7 August 1821.

George's critics overplayed a strong hand. A good deal of the animosity against the Prince was politically inspired, and it was in this spirit that *The Times* could dismiss him as 'a hard-drinking, swearing man who at all times would prefer a girl and a bottle to politics and a sermon'. But there was more to George than that. When he was near sober, his conversation was fascinating and full of amusing anecdote. He had a good memory and was an excellent mimic. George (Beau) Brummell said that he could have been the best comic actor in Europe. He was by far the most intelligent of the Hanoverians and could hold his own in the Sublime Society of Beefsteaks, to which he was elected in 1784.

But George's greatest claim to fame was as a man of style, a man of taste. Before George, the Hanoverians had been decidedly philistine. Almost as if they expected to be sent back to Germany at any moment they had virtually camped in the rambling and uncomfortable buildings left by the Stuarts. George was determined to create palaces which would rival any in Europe. Styles varied from the 'Gothick' restoration of Windsor Castle, the 'rustick' of the Royal Lodge to the extraordinary 'Oriental' of the Brighton Pavilion. Of course it was easy to make fun of the Brighton Pavilion; William Cobbett wrote: 'Take a square box, take a large Norfolk turnip and put the turnip on the top of the box. Then take four turnips of half the size and put them on the corners of the box. Then take a considerable number of bulbs of the crown-imperial and put them pretty promiscuously about the top of the box. Then stand off. There! That's a Kremlin.'

An illustration taken from *Views of the Royal Pavilion, Brighton* by John Nash, which was published in 1826. The picture shows the west-facing King's Apartments with the Household Apartments above them.

Despite Cobbett's jibe, there can be no doubt that the Brighton Pavilion was a success. The mixture of domes and minarets, the Chinese furniture and the lotus and dragon chandeliers could have produced a palace of quite hideous vulgarity. But the Pavilion's exuberance always stops short of vulgarity and it was the personal sensitivity of George IV which prevented this outcome. George did not follow fashions, he set them. One of his most important discoveries was of the seaside resort and the life-style which went with it. The style evolved; in the early days Brighton was a byword for almost every kind of wildness but later the Prince enjoyed a quiet, almost domestic, existence there. Perhaps the change was symbolised by the abandonment of multi-coloured 'peacock' fashions in favour of the smart black, sombre dress pioneered by George and Brummell in the 1790s. In 1800 Mrs Fitzherbert returned to live with the man whom she regarded as her lawful husband, cut down his drinking and nursed him back to health when he was stricken with inflammation of the stomach.

Politically, George was not to be trusted. As a young man one of his closest companions was Charles James Fox; George had even applauded when Fox had strutted in the uniform of the American rebels. But George's Whiggism was really a means of annoying his father. He supported Fox because Fox was an enemy of William Pitt and Pitt was his father's choice as premier. Politics was a game which became deadly earnest after 1793. The Prince came to the conclusion that the type of Whiggery dispensed by Fox could lead to anarchy and revolution. George had made countless promises to the Whigs but as soon as he gained any real power he told them that they could expect nothing from him and that he intended to keep his father's Tory ministers in office. As King, George came to share his father's views that the concession of the right of Roman Catholics to sit in Parliament would involve a violation

Cruikshank's cartoon satirising George's physical and moral deterioration from being a handsome, regal Prince of Wales to a bloated, debauched Prince Regent.

of the sacred coronation oath. By the late 1820s, the Whig of the 1780s had become an ultra-Tory.

Whigs like Lord Grey never forgave this 'betrayal' of their cause, yet George was not a vicious man. Perhaps he was too worn out even by the time he became Regent for one to expect determined stands. George was a weak and vacillating ruler. He was untrustworthy because he did not like scenes, because he was lazy and because he always took the easy way out. In 1829 he appeared to accept Wellington's decision that the government must grant Catholic Emancipation and then, under pressure from the Duke of Cumberland, denied that he had ever given his consent. Even in his worst moments there was still a streak of kindness in George IV. He might be ferocious in his general pronouncements but it was a different matter when it came to individual cases. When Robert Peel became Home Secretary he was amazed to find himself being woken up at 2 a.m. with messages from the King urging him to reprieve criminals due to be executed the next morning.

George was forty-eight when he became Prince Regent. He put on great spectacles to celebrate his new power; later there were banquets and triumphal arches to celebrate the Allied victory over Napoleon and entertainments for visiting sovereigns. When it came to planning things like this, George forgot his ailments, overcame his laziness and mastered every detail. His coronation was probably the most elaborate of all time, the ultimate in regal splendour, with the new King looking like 'some gorgeous bird of paradise'. In the following year George made enormously successful state visits to Dublin and Edinburgh where he paraded up Princes Street wearing the Stuart tartan. The visit to Ireland, the most rebellious part of the United Kingdom, was a particularly bold step. There must have been something a little special about a man whose presence could make an old Irishman declare, 'I was a rebel to Old King George in '98 but, by God I would die a thousand deaths for his son.'

George was at his best on such occasions. He could behave with superb royal dignity and at least temporarily remove the bad impression his other actions created. In the days of the Regency, *The Morning Post* could still describe George as 'an Adonis of Loveliness' but the picture depended on cosmetics and corsets. The hectic style of the first two years of the reign did not last. George was an old man well before he was sixty. He did not sleep well and his remaining energy was sapped by the large doses of laudanum he took with his brandy. George became a very expensive recluse living at Windsor Castle, his mind filled with fan-

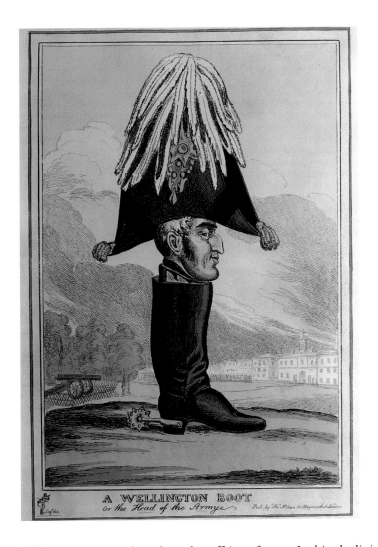

'A Wellington Boot, or, the Head of the Army': a contemporary cartoon of the Duke of Wellington in the boot to which he gave his name. Wellington not only orchestrated the defeat of Napoleon's armies, he also became a leading politician – and was frustrated by the vacillations of George IV.

ciful building projects rather than the affairs of state. In his declining years, the King was surrounded by a group of elderly former mistresses and dominated by his sinister doctor and confidant, Sir William Knighton. Visitors from London found the scene pathetic or just plain boring. Occasionally the King pretended that he had played a promi-nent part in the battle of Waterloo; no one could tell if it was a joke to annoy the Duke of Wellington or whether George IV, like his father, was going mad. It was a world of fantasy, of 'might have been'; in a way George had been a great man but the sad thing was that his last years were haunted by the realisation that he might have been – indeed should have been – very much greater.

WILLIAM IV *r.* 1830-37

*I*T WAS NOT UNTIL AFTER THE DEATHS of Princess Charlotte in 1818 and the Duke of York in 1827 that people began to pay much attention to William Henry, Duke of Clarence. As third son of George III and Queen Charlotte, it seemed so unlikely that he would ever be King that no one attempted to teach him to behave in a regal way. Unlike George IV, William had been given a job to do. At the age of thirteen he became a midshipman in the Royal Navy. William enjoyed his life at sea and soon became a competent if rather severe officer. His tastes were those of a sailor, his language strong and his opinions forthright. William was certainly an honest man but no one could call him sophisticated. He followed his eldest brother in rebelling against their father and actually tried to become a Member of Parliament in the opposition interest. Unlike the Prince of Wales, William was not the man to wound his father by some brilliant epigram nor could he put the same intensity of bitterness into the quarrel. William was liked by most members of the royal family but the general opinion was that he was rather a fool – 'Silly Billy' was the inevitable nickname.

From 1791 to 1811 William lived in irregular but very domestic bliss with Mrs Jordan, a famous London actress. The Prince's mistress was thirty, stout and was to be the mother of a large family of Fitzclarences. Perhaps William was genuinely happy in these years but he was certainly angry that no one thought of asking him to take command of a fleet, or even a ship, throughout the long struggle against Revolutionary France. The Duke's tactlessness was frequently revealed in his speeches in the House of Lords. During a discussion on the slave trade he asserted: 'The promoters of abolition are either fanatics or hypocrites

Opposite: A portrait of William IV by John Simpson. Apprenticed to the Royal Navy at the age of thirteen, the Duke of Clarence, nicknamed 'Silly Billy' by the royal family, had never expected to rule.

and in one of these classes I rank Mr Wilberforce.' The rest of the speech was drowned by cries of 'Withdraw'.

In the royal scramble to marry and produce an heir to the throne after the death of Princess Charlotte in 1818, William's prize was Adelaide of Saxe-Coburg-Meiningen, an excellent wife but plain, evangelical and much concerned with 'the end'. She must have been dull after Mrs Jordan and, unlike that prolific lady, none of her children lived more than a few hours. As he grew older, William became increasingly eccentric. In 1827 he was appointed High Admiral of England, an entirely honorific post, and caused great scandal by hoisting his standard at Plymouth and taking a squadron to sea in defiance of orders from the Admiralty. Despite his views on slavery, William was more progressive than George IV and after 1827 he was assiduously courted by the Whigs and the more liberal Tories. He was a strong supporter of Catholic Emancipation and intervened in a debate in the House of Lords to deliver a very bitter attack on the Protestant champion, Ernest, Duke of Cumberland. Opinions differed about William. Charles Grenville dismissed him as 'a mountebank bidding fair to be a maniac', but for most people in June 1830 he was an unknown quantity.

William IV heard that he was King on the morning of 26 June 1830 when Sir Henry Halford, physician to George IV, rode out to Bushey to announce his master's death. William had taken care to live to this day – gargling two gallons of water every morning and wearing huge galoshes to guard against chills. The new King could scarcely contain his glee. William was an excitable man and, in the first few days, behaved extremely wildly. On the first day of his reign, this bluff, hearty-looking man of sixty-four was seen racing through London in an open carriage, grinning all over his face, frequently removing his hat to reveal his bullet-head and bowing low to any of his new subjects who appeared interested. He allowed himself to be kissed by street-walkers and was liable to stop his carriage and ask anyone who looked moderately respectable if they wanted a lift. It must have been a hideous experience for courtiers who had modelled themselves on the aloof and remote George IV. William's habit of spitting – frequently and copiously – when in public was considered as indicating a lack of gentility.

William's delight in his new position was summed up when he asked, 'Who is Silly Billy now?' as the Privy Council lined up to kneel before their new master. The King had been practising his new signature 'William R' for several months. There was a backlog of literally

La Promenade en Famille. — a Sketch from Life.

A Gillray cartoon from 1797 called *'La Promenade en Famille'*, lampooning the private life of William, Duke of Clarence. For twenty years he lived with Mrs Jordan, and she bore him several children.

thousands of documents from the previous reign. The new monarch kept on signing 'William R' far into the night – with a basin of warm water to ease the pain of chalk stones in his hands. But William soon showed himself to be more than an amiable old fool. To the horror of his court, he insisted on the simplest of coronations. He would not hear of the new robes and vast banquets indulged in by George IV. William was adamant that his coronation would cost only a tenth of the expense incurred in 1821. When some old-fashioned peers threatened a boycott, the King replied, 'I anticipate from that greater convenience of room and less heat.' Royal economy was popular with hard-pressed tax-payers and even the King's detractors had to admit that he was received with great acclamation.

Queen Adelaide was in constant dread of revolution and prayed that she would behave as well as Marie Antoinette when taken to the guillotine. William, on the other hand, looked at the future with greater

Adelaide of Saxe-Coburg-Meiningen, wife of William IV. Adelaide made an excellent wife, but she was regarded as plain and was dull compared to William's mistress.

confidence. A Whig government committed to sweeping changes came to power in November 1830. Wellington warned the King that Lord Grey was an 'ill-tempered violent man' but William got on well with his new premier. He assured Grey that he had 'complete confidence in your integrity, judgement, decision and experience'. In April 1831 Grey asked the King to dissolve Parliament so that the Whigs could secure a larger majority to carry their proposals for Parliamentary reform. As there had been an election less than a year earlier, the King could have refused and the Reform Bill of 1832 would have been postponed – perhaps very dangerously.

But William accepted Grey's request. Court officials told the King that he could not go to Westminster at short notice. There would be no time for the guards to line the streets or for the royal grooms to plait the manes of the horses for the state coach. William turned to Grey and said, 'My Lord, I'll go if I go in a hackney coach.' The King walked into the House of Lords, his crown on crooked, and read the speech of dissolution. He returned to the Palace through cheering crowds. 'Well done, old boy,' they cried, 'served 'em right.'

William did not long remain the hero of progressives and was soon to be accused of tricking Grey and going back on his promise to create peers to get the Reform Bill through the Lords. After his initial enthusiasm, William was finding the pace of reform rather too hot. In November 1834 he abruptly dismissed the Whigs from office and persuaded Peel to become prime minister. The experiment failed and by the following spring he had to submit to the humiliation of asking the Whigs to return. The two politicians William most loathed were Brougham and Lord John Russell. He said of Russell, 'If you will answer for his death, I will answer for his damnation.'

The pleasures of kingship which William had so eagerly embraced were further embittered by quarrels within the royal family. The heir to the throne was the King's niece Victoria, daughter of Edward, Duke of Kent. The Duke had died in 1820 and between the Duchess and the

King there was much bad feeling. Victoria was not allowed to come to court because her mother said it was a hot-bed of vice. Although the King was not a man to mince his words, even in the presence of young girls, the charge was absurd. The King responded by circulating crude stories about the Duchess of Kent's relationship with Sir John Conroy, the Controller of her household. In 1836 the Duchess took over a large suite of rooms in Kensington Palace without the King's permission. William was furious. If he died now, Victoria would be too young to rule without her mother as Regent. At a public dinner, attended by over a hundred guests, William said that he hoped his life would be spared long enough to prevent such a calamity. His wish was granted; he lived for a month after Victoria's eighteenth birthday. William IV died on 20 June 1837, muttering 'The Church, the Church' – a remark utterly out of keeping with the rest of his life.

Whig supporters of Lord Grey's Reform Bill, designed to reform Parliament, attack the 'rotten boroughs' tree. William IV watches from a safe distance.

The Reformers' Attack on the Old Rotten Tree; or, the Foul Nests of the Cormorants in Danger. Pub. by E. King Chancery lane.

VICTORIA *r. 1837–1901*

QUEEN VICTORIA WAS BORN AT Kensington Palace in London on 24 May 1819, the daughter of Edward, Duke of Kent, and Princess Victoire, the widow of the Prince of Leiningen. The Duke of Kent was the fourth son of the reigning monarch, George III. Princess Victoire was the daughter of the Duke of Saxe-Coburg, and the sister of Leopold of Saxe-Coburg, who afterwards became King Leopold I of Belgium – Queen Victoria's uncle, to whom she turned so frequently for advice on political and other matters until his death in 1865. The Duke and Duchess of Kent wished to name their baby Victoria, but the Prince Regent – the future George IV – insisted that she be named Alexandrina after her godfather, Tsar Alexander I of Russia, and she was therefore christened Alexandrina Victoria. Her father died when she was eight months old. His three elder brothers had no surviving children, and when, on the death of George IV in 1830, the Duke of Clarence succeeded him as King William IV, Princess Victoria, at the age of eleven, became heir presumptive to the throne.

After her father's death, her mother, the Duchess of Kent, had fallen under the influence of the Controller of her household, Sir John Conroy, who was an ambitious Irish officer. Conroy was generally thought to be the Duchess's lover, and as he took complete control of her household and of Princess Victoria, it was rumoured that he was planning to become the power behind the throne in the event of William IV dying before Princess Victoria was eighteen and the Duchess of Kent becoming Regent. Conroy organised a number of 'journeys' on which the Duchess of Kent took Princess Victoria travelling in semi-regal pomp through the West Midlands and the north

Opposite: Princess Victoria in 1833 at the age of fourteen. After her father's death, Victoria's mother fell under the influence of Sir John Conroy, who hoped to wield power behind the throne if William IV died before Victoria's eighteenth birthday.

of England. William IV was annoyed at these tours, and took steps to curtail the honours which were to be paid to the Duchess and to Princess Victoria.

But Conroy's hopes of exercising power during a regency were disappointed. Princess Victoria reached the age of eighteen in May 1837, twenty-seven days before William IV died on 20 June; and as she disliked Conroy, and resented his control, her first act as Queen was to free herself from his influence and from her mother's. Conroy was excluded from court, to the great distress of the Duchess.

During her first years on the throne, Queen Victoria's closest confidants were her governess, the German Baroness von Lehzen, and the prime minister, Lord Melbourne. Melbourne, who was aged fifty-eight in 1837, was a Whig of the old school, whose attitude to the great campaigns for the reform of the political and social systems was summed up in the phrase which he used whenever any reform was suggested: 'Why not leave it alone?'

A CABINET LECTURE.

He showed no concern over the sufferings of the poor in the mines, factories and workhouses which were causing great social unrest. A symptom of this unrest was the attempt to assassinate, or at least to assault, the Queen when she was driving in her carriage in London in 1840. Two similar attempts were made in 1842, and other attempts in 1849, 1850, 1872 and 1882.

Melbourne's charm, his perfect manners and his gallantry to the ladies had made him the centre of London society, and he developed a respectful and avuncular intimacy with the Queen. He delighted in the company and friendship of his young female sovereign; and her attitude to him is shown by such diary entries as 'Lord Melbourne rode near me the whole time', 'Lord Melbourne sat near me the whole evening', 'I am so fond of Lord Melbourne'. She accepted his opinion on all matters from politics to the comparative merits of Shakespeare's plays.

This led to a political crisis in 1839, when Melbourne resigned after a defeat in Parliament, and Queen Victoria invited Sir Robert Peel, the

'A Cabinet Lecture': Queen Victoria with Lord Melbourne in 1840.

Opposite: The coronation of the eighteen-year-old Queen Victoria in Westminster Abbey in 1838, painted by John Martin.

Following pages: Sir David Wilkie's 1838 painting of Queen Victoria's first Crown Council session, in Kensington Palace. Seated in front of the Victoria is Prime Minister Lord Melbourne, while the Duke of Wellington stands by the column.

Conservative leader, to form a government. Peel insisted that the Queen's Whig Ladies of the Bedchamber should be replaced, in accordance with the usual practice, by Tory ladies; and when the Queen refused to agree, Peel refused to form a government, and Melbourne and the Whigs returned to office for another two years. Queen Victoria's victory was only temporary, because never again did she challenge the principle that the officers of the royal household should change with the government.

In the same year, the Queen became very unpopular as a result of the case of Lady Flora Hastings. Lady Flora, one of the Queen's ladies-in-waiting, suffered from a cancerous growth on the liver which made her appear to be pregnant, and as she was unmarried this gave rise to scandal. The Queen was very ready to believe the worst, because on one occasion Lady Flora had been seen alone in a carriage with Sir John Conroy. Lady Flora was virtually compelled, against her protests, to submit to a medical examination, which proved that she was a virgin, and a few months later she died of the cancer. Public opinion strongly condemned the conduct of the Queen and court in the affair, and Queen Victoria was hissed on the racecourse at Ascot, and greeted with shouts of 'Mrs Melbourne'.

As soon as the festivities of the coronation of June 1838 were over, the Queen's advisers considered the question of her marriage. When one of the candidates, her cousin Prince Albert of Saxe-Coburg-Gotha, visited London in 1839, the Queen fell in love with him. Prince Albert was three months younger than Queen Victoria. His father was Duke of a German state which was about the size of Worcestershire. When Prince Albert was seven years old, his father divorced his mother on a charge of adultery with an officer at his court, and she was sent to live in Switzerland on a pension and forbidden to see her children. This subsequent accusation of adultery against his mother appears to be the only real ground for the rumour which arose many years later that Prince Albert's father was not the Duke, but another officer – a Jew – with whom his mother was alleged to have had an affair. Prince Albert always remembered his mother with great affection. He did not immediately reciprocate Queen Victoria's feelings for him – perhaps he was never as deeply in love with her as she was with him – but a strong affection for her, as well as a sense of mission, made him willingly agree to marry her. The wedding took place in London in February 1840, when both bride and bridegroom were aged twenty. It was very unpopular in certain

Opposite: The handsome and morally upstanding Prince Albert, Victoria's beloved Prince Consort, in a portrait from the studio of Franz Xavier Winterhalter. Their marriage was a long and happy one, and Victoria never really recovered from his death.

quarters. To Queen Victoria's great indignation, Parliament made diffi-culties about voting a suitable allowance for Prince Albert and about granting him precedence over the Queen's surviving uncles; and Radical journalists and ballad-writers jeered at the 'pauper Prince' who had come begging to England, and instead of being sent to the work-house, like other beggars, had been given the hand of England's Queen.

The marriage was very happy. Now that the royal archives are open to inspection it is known — which no one suspected at the time — that Queen Victoria and Prince Albert sometimes quarrelled about such matters as the upbringing of the children and the influence which Baroness von Lehzen still held over the Queen. But these were unim-portant incidents in a very happy relationship. They had nine children — in 1840, Victoria, the Princess Royal, who married the future Emperor of Germany, Frederick III; in 1841, Edward, Prince of Wales, the future King Edward VII; and three boys and four girls followed.

Prince Albert was considered to be very handsome, and his arrival had caused considerable excitement among the ladies of the court; but he showed no interest in them. His attitude had repercussions far beyond the family circle. At the beginning of the nineteenth century a great moral revival had been launched by Wilberforce and his Society for the Suppression of Vice, as part of the campaign to inculcate reli-gion and discipline among the working classes as an antidote to the Radical and free-thinking propaganda which followed the French Revolution. At first the gambling, heavy drinking and sexual licence common in aristocratic society continued unabated; and although the aristocracy made every attempt to present a moral face in public while they sinned in private, their vices, and those of the royal Dukes, were well known, and featured prominently in Radical propaganda. Under Queen Victoria and Prince Albert the royal family became moral, and set an example which was followed, at least to some extent, in society as well as among the middle classes. Both Queen Victoria and Prince Albert strongly disapproved of any sexual misconduct, especially if practised by their sons or ministers, though they reacted differently. Queen Victoria sadly resigned herself to the fact that men have love affairs; but Prince Albert reacted with almost hysterical indignation when he heard that his son the Prince of Wales had had an affair with an actress, or that the Foreign Secretary, Lord Palmerston, had tried to enter the bedroom of one of the ladies-in-waiting in the middle of the night at Windsor Castle.

Albert also influenced Victoria's attitude towards social problems. Her first mentor, the Whig Lord Melbourne, had advised her not to read Charles Dickens's *Oliver Twist* because it dealt with paupers, criminals and other unpleasant subjects with which she should not be troubled; but Albert invited Lord Ashley – later Lord Shaftesbury – to the palace and told him how moved he and the Queen had been at Ashley's revelations in Parliament about the sufferings of the children who worked in the mines. Ashley invited Prince Albert to preside at meetings of the committee of the Labourer's Friend Society; and when, despite all the apprehensions of the government and court, Prince Albert attended the meeting and delighted the other members of the committee by his interest, Ashley noted that this was the way to defeat the Chartists and the socialists. As well as showing

interest in plans for model workers' houses and the relief of poverty, Prince Albert interested himself in projects for the encouragement of trade and industry. His most ambitious venture in this field was the Great International Exhibition of 1851, for which he was chiefly responsible. It encountered considerable opposition, both from those who objected to the felling of the trees in Hyde Park and the interference with the riding in Rotten Row, and from patriots who resented the influx of foreigners into Britain; but it was a great success.

The fall of Melbourne's government in 1841 brought the Tories to power. The Queen was very distressed to lose Melbourne, and said so frankly to her new prime minister, Peel; but she soon abandoned her practice of writing to Melbourne about state affairs, and partly thanks to Prince Albert's influence she came to have a high regard for Peel. She supported the policy of Peel's Foreign Secretary, Lord Aberdeen, of a

Queen Victoria and the Prince Consort visiting King Louis Philippe of France at Chateau d'Eu during 1845.

diplomatic *rapprochement* with France, and played her part in it when she visited the French King, Louis Philippe, at the Château d'Eu at Tréport in 1843, this being the first time that a reigning English sovereign had met a foreign sovereign since the reign of Henry VIII. In the following year King Louis Philippe paid a return visit to England. In the next decade Queen Victoria similarly exchanged state visits with the French Emperor, Napoleon III.

When the Whigs returned to power in 1846, with Lord John Russell as prime minister and Palmerston as Foreign Secretary, the Queen and Prince Albert soon came into conflict with Palmerston. The first clash came in connection with the civil war in Portugal in 1846–7. and more serious disagreements arose during and after the revolutions which broke out in so many countries of Europe in 1848. Palmerston, who had begun his political career as a junior minister in a Tory government, had not basically changed his political opinions at the age of sixty; he was still profoundly conservative, anti-revolutionary and anti-democratic. But he was convinced of the superiority of the British system of constitutional monarchy over the absolutist monarchies of the continent; he was eager to embarrass and weaken foreign governments in order to improve the relative position of Britain; and he was playing for Radical support in British home politics. He therefore gave moral support to revolutionary Liberal, and even Radical, movements throughout Europe. Queen Victoria and Prince Albert, on the other hand, believed in solidarity with the sovereigns of Europe, many of whom were their friends and relations, and favoured a policy of preserving peace and avoiding revolution by international co-operation between rulers. They were too logical, broad-minded and cosmopolitan to share the attitude of Whigs like Russell and Palmerston, who, on hearing that the Austrian military authorities had flogged rebellious patriots in Italy and Hungary, could exclaim in all sincerity, 'The Austrians are really the greatest brutes that ever called themselves by the undeserved name of civilised men', almost on the same day on which they themselves authorised the wholesale flogging of peasants who had risen in revolt against British rule in the Ionian Isles. Queen Victoria and Prince Albert could not see what right the British government had to protest against the suppression of revolution in the territories of foreign kings who had never protested to Britain against the suppression of revolution in Ireland or the sentences passed on Chartist rioters. They did not share the enthusiasm of nearly the whole of the British people for Garibaldi; and when

Opposite: The Great International Exhibition, which took place in Hyde Park in 1851, was one of Prince Albert's most ambitious and most successful projects. The Prince Consort was deeply interested in the arts, manufacture and commerce as well as in social issues.

Queen Victoria visits wounded troops during the Crimean War (1854–6). Victoria was proud of her noble troops fighting in the Crimea and showed genuine concern for their suffering.

Garibaldi visited England in 1864, Queen Victoria was indignant that aristocrats and society hostesses should acclaim and fall in love with a revolutionary Radical. 'Brave and honest though he is,' she logically commented, 'he has ever been a revolutionist leader.'

The Queen, with Prince Albert acting as her private secretary, insisted on her constitutional right to have all Palmerston's despatches to foreign governments submitted to her before they were sent off. She and Prince Albert often altered Palmerston's text, in order to delete or soften the most provocative passages. Palmerston therefore sometimes sent off despatches without submitting them to the Queen. In the summer of 1850 Queen Victoria and Prince Albert asked Lord John Russell to dismiss Palmerston from the Foreign Office. Russell told them that this was impossible because of Palmerston's great popularity in the House of Commons and in the country; but the Queen and Prince bided their time. In December 1851 Palmerston for once made a move which was unpopular with the majority of Englishmen, especially his Radical supporters, by congratulating Louis Napoleon Bonaparte – the future Emperor Napoleon III – on his *coup d'état* in France. Queen Victoria and Prince Albert seized their chance, and persuaded Russell to dismiss Palmerston from the Foreign Office. Within six weeks Palmerston had brought down Russell's government in the House of Commons, and a year after he left the Foreign Office he returned to office as Home Secretary in Lord Aberdeen's coalition government.

In 1854 the Crimean War broke out – the first major European war for forty years – when Britain and France declared war on Russia in support of Turkey. For nearly a year before the declaration of war, the prime minister, Lord Aberdeen, tried to avoid it by pursuing a conciliatory policy; Palmerston, in the Cabinet, urged a tougher policy that he believed was the only way of deterring the Russians from attacking Turkey. Prince Albert supported Aberdeen's policy, and drafted a memorandum containing a plan that he believed would prevent war. Although the memorandum was secret, Prince Albert's pacific policy and his opposition to Palmerston became generally known, and made him unpopular at a time when there was a great clamour for war with Russia and for Palmerston to lead it. The rumour spread that Prince Albert was a Russian spy and had been arrested and sent to the Tower of London after the authorities had intercepted his communications with the Russians. Pamphlets were published attacking him, and pointing out that the husband of a reigning queen could be put on trial for high treason against her; and a ballad, 'Lovely Albert', circulated in the streets of London:

> It is rumoured over Britain's isle
> That A… is in the Tower;
> The Postmen some suspicion had,
> And opened the two letters;
> 'Twas a pity sad the German lad
> Should not have known much better.

As the news reached England of the set-backs and incompetence in the Crimea, public opinion maintained insistently that only Palmerston could win the war, and the Queen was compelled, very reluctantly, to accept him as prime minister in February 1855. Although the efficiency of the army in the Crimea did not noticeably improve after Palmerston came to power, the war was won and, thanks chiefly to Palmerston's firm attitude at the Peace Congress, Russia was compelled to cede territory to Turkey and to relinquish the right to maintain a fleet in the Black Sea. Once war had been declared, Queen Victoria had supported it enthusiastically; she showed great concern over the sufferings of the soldiers in the Crimea, and wrote: 'I feel so *proud* of my dear noble troops.' She approved of Palmerston's conduct of the peace negotiations, and formed a more favourable view of him as prime minister than she had done when he was Foreign Secretary, not least because he succeeded in 1857 in persuading Parliament to agree at last to her wish that the title of Prince Consort should be bestowed on Prince Albert. There were signs of the old tensions in 1864, when Palmerston and his Foreign Secretary, Lord Russell, supported Denmark in the German-Danish war, while Queen Victoria sympathised with Prussia; but when Palmerston died in office in 1865, the Queen commented: 'We had, God knows! terrible trouble with him about Foreign Affairs. Still, as Prime Minister he managed affairs at home well, and behaved to me well. But I *never* liked him.'

In December 1861 Queen Victoria suffered a great personal tragedy when Prince Albert died of typhoid fever at the age of forty-two. A few days before his death he had made an important diplomatic intervention. On the outbreak of the American Civil War, the British government's sympathies were with the South, because although British public opinion had previously supported the campaign for the abolition of slavery in the United States, Palmerston and Russell could not resist taking advantage of the situation to weaken the United States, which they regarded as a growing menace to British international power, and to assist a process which might lead to the United States being permanently divided into two nations. A few months after the outbreak of the Civil War, a US warship stopped and boarded a British merchant ship, *The Trent*, in the Caribbean Sea and removed two envoys of the Southern Confederacy who were travelling on diplomatic business to Europe. The British government demanded that the two envoys be released, and when President Lincoln's government refused, public indignation in both Britain and the United States reached such a pitch that war seemed probable. The US minister in London afterwards stated that he believed that if the Atlantic cable, which was laid a few years later, had been in existence in 1861, war would have been inevitable, but that as despatches took a month to travel between London and Washington, there was time for passions to cool. At the height of the crisis the Prince Consort, though seriously ill, rose from his bed to alter the wording of a draft despatch from the British government to the United States so as to make it less provocative, and to make it easier for the US government to accept the British demands. The US gave way and released the two envoys, and thus avoided a war between Britain and the United States that might have altered the course of history.

Queen Victoria was prostrated by Prince Albert's death. It was an accepted convention at the time that widows should display their grief and show signs of mourning in a way that would seem morbid today; but the Queen's reaction seemed excessive even by the standards of 1861. She withdrew into complete seclusion, and refused her ministers' requests that she should open Parliament in person and show herself at least occasionally to her subjects (though throughout this period, from the very first days after Prince Albert's death, she insisted on reading all the diplomatic despatches and on carrying out her constitutional duties in the privacy of her closet). She spent much time in the Scottish Highlands at her house at Balmoral, which she and Prince Albert had acquired in 1847 and where they had spent happy times together.

It was during the decade after Prince Albert's death that Queen Victoria came under the influence of John Brown, a Scottish servant. Brown's blunt manner and kindly concern pleased the Queen, who did not resent it when he addressed her as 'woman' as he put a scarf around her shoulders to keep her warm or bullied her into taking care of her health. Queen Victoria believed, as Prince Albert had done, that the working class, who showed their loyalty to the throne without observing the accepted conventions of court etiquette, were far more worthy than the arrogant and often immoral aristocracy with whom, to her regret, her son the Prince of Wales associated. Her ideal of government was a benevolent sovereign ruling constitutionally over a contented and loyal people; and she thought that this ideal was thwarted both by a selfish, pleasure-loving aristocracy and by Radical agitators with their belief in democracy.

The Queen's friendship with Brown caused resentment among her family and courtiers, and stories spread in society, and were published in foreign newspapers, that the Queen had secretly married Brown. References to 'Mrs Brown', meaning the Queen, were common at

An early photograph showing Queen Victoria and her faithful Scottish servant, John Brown, at Balmoral in 1862. Her intense reliance on him after the loss of Albert gave rise to the disrespectful nickname 'Mrs Brown' among London society.

society dinner tables in London. The Queen's isolation was resented. Radical spokesmen publicly stated that she was not earning the money that the state paid her, and some of them, especially the prominent Liberal politician Sir Charles Dilke, spoke in favour of abolishing the monarchy and replacing it with a republic. The campaign for a republic caused some stir in 1871, but soon died out.

The last thirty-five years of Queen Victoria's reign were a period of struggle between the new Liberal Party and the Conservatives. The forces of Liberalism were led by William Ewart Gladstone, who had begun his political life as a Tory, but at the age of fifty, when he was Chancellor of the Exchequer in Palmerston's government, had developed Liberal and almost Radical ideas that aroused his prime minister's opposition and alarm. Queen Victoria's relations with Gladstone were worse than with any of her other prime ministers. His sincere devotion to the throne and to the Queen as a woman was expressed in a pompous and impersonal way, and although he was very eager to win her approval, he failed completely to do so. As in the case of her hostility to Palmerston in earlier years, her personal dislike of Gladstone was not as important a factor as her political opposition to the cause which he represented. On the great issues that dominated British politics in the last quarter of the century – the extension of the Parliamentary franchise, the limitation of the power of the House of Lords, social reform, home rule for Ireland, and the new, aggressive Conservative imperialist policy abroad – Queen Victoria strongly sympathised with the Conservatives and disapproved of Gladstone and the Liberals.

In 1868 Benjamin Disraeli became prime minister, and though he held office for only nine months, he established a very close relationship with the Queen that became more intimate after he returned to office in 1874 for his second term as premier, which lasted for six years. He told a friend: 'Everyone likes flattery, and when you come to royalty, you should lay it on with a trowel.' He spoke and wrote to the Queen in the most exaggerated and fulsome language; but it was not too exaggerated or fulsome for Queen Victoria's liking. She became genuinely attached to Disraeli, paid him the signal honour of visiting him in his private house in the country, and was deeply unhappy when he fell from power in 1880. When he died in the next year, she wrote to his private secretary: 'Dear Lord Rowton, I cannot write in the third person at this terrible moment when I can scarcely see for my fast falling tears.'

Disraeli gratified the Queen in 1876 by persuading Parliament to agree to grant her the title of Empress of India. Queen Victoria relished the title, and showed great interest in her Indian Empire. At the time of the Indian Mutiny in 1857 she had been one of the very few people in Britain who did not join in the clamour for indiscriminate slaughter of Indians in revenge for the murder of British women and children at Cawnpore and elsewhere; and she and Prince Albert supported the Governor-General of India, Lord Canning, when he aroused a storm of indignation in Britain and among the British residents in India by his proclamation in which he urged the commanders in the field to show some restraint in the number of executions. The Queen was very conscious of her duties to her Indian subjects, and here, as in Britain, she believed in her ideal of paternalistic government. She always expressed her indignation when she encountered signs of racial prejudice by British officials in India. In the last years of her life she angered her courtiers by her intimate friendship with an Indian servant; and her disapproval of the attitude of the Boers towards the blacks in South Africa was another reason for her patriotic and belligerent attitude during the Boer War.

It was during Disraeli's second term of office that the Queen developed her deep dislike of Gladstone, with whom she had been on reasonably good terms during Gladstone's first premiership in 1868–74. She strongly approved of Disraeli's imperialist foreign policy and his support of Turkey against Russia during the Russo-Turkish war of 1876–7, and she applauded his success at the Congress of Berlin in 1878, when he thwarted Russia's plan to liberate the Balkan provinces of Turkey. This policy, which involved supporting the Sultan's oppressive regime in the Balkans against the Christians in Bulgaria and Herzegovina who were fighting for their freedom, outraged the feelings of Gladstone and the 'Nonconformist conscience' of his Liberal supporters. Gladstone and the Liberals proclaimed that England, in her foreign policy, must never support a cause which was morally wrong; Disraeli proudly claimed that his foreign policy was 'as selfish as patriotism'. The Queen thought Gladstone and his followers were not merely misguided, but traitors to their country.

During Gladstone's last three terms as premier – in 1880–85, 1886 and 1892–4 – his relations with the Queen, to his great regret, were very strained. On most occasions her conduct was correct and courteous, but there were occasions when she administered personal slights and incivilities, and she privately passed on confidential documents of Gladstone's government to the Conservative Leader of the Opposition, Lord Salisbury. In 1885 she administered a public rebuke to Gladstone when she sent him an uncoded telegram – which was delivered to him by a local station-master, and became public knowledge – in which she condemned his government for not acting sufficiently promptly and energetically to relieve General Gordon at Khartoum, after she and the great majority of her subjects had been shocked by the news of Gordon's death at the hands of the Mahdi's nationalist rebels in the Sudan.

The Queen's Conservative and imperialist views coincided with those of a substantial proportion – at most times a majority – of the British people and a Conservative government under Lord Salisbury

Opposite: Victoria accompanied by Benjamin Disraeli, her favourite prime minister. As a result of his influence, Parliament granted the Queen the title of Empress of India, which pleased her greatly.

Queen Victoria's procession outside St Paul's Cathedral during her Diamond Jubilee celebrations in June 1897.

was in power during twelve of the last fifteen years of her reign. Her former unpopularity disappeared, and she was revered and almost worshipped by the public. Her Jubilee on the fiftieth anniversary of her accession in 1887 was the occasion for great national celebrations. On 23 September 1896 she noted in her diary that she had reigned one day longer than George III or any previous English sovereign; and on 20 June 1897 her Diamond Jubilee was celebrated amid scenes of enthusiasm which completely eclipsed those of ten years earlier, and which culminated in the Queen's visit to St Paul's Cathedral in London on 22 June, when she was cheered by a vast crowd. 'I was much moved and gratified,' wrote the Queen.

During her remaining years, Britain engaged in the last of the many wars of the Victorian era. General Kitchener's success in destroying the Mahdi's successor and avenging Gordon in the Sudan in 1898, and his diplomatic triumph over the French at Fashoda, had delighted the Queen; and she enthusiastically supported the Boer War in 1899. Although distressed by the British defeats in South Africa in the opening stages of the war, she refused to permit any defeatist talk at court. 'In this house', she declared, 'we are not interested in the possibilities of defeat; they do not exist.' Before her death, the tide had definitely turned in favour of Britain in South Africa, after the relief of Mafeking and Ladysmith in the summer of 1900.

Queen Victoria died at her house at Osborne in the Isle of Wight, after a short illness, on 22 January 1901, at the

Celebrations in Bombay to mark Victoria's Golden Jubilee in 1887. A triumphal arch was raised, together with a statue of the Empress. Victoria was genuinely popular in India and took her responsibilities to her Indian subjects seriously.

age of eighty-one. None of the court officials had any personal experience of the measures which were to be taken at the death of a sovereign and the accession of a new king, and her death caused consternation among nearly all her subjects, as no one under the age of seventy could remember living under another monarch.

Crowds watch as the Royal Yacht conveys the body of Queen Victoria from the Isle of Wight to the mainland in January 1901.

THE ROYAL ARMS
1707-1837

THE ROYAL ARMS WERE ALTERED TO reflect the union of England and Scotland under James I. The arms of the two countries were placed side by side in the first and last quarters, France was assigned the second quarter and Ireland stayed put. No alteration was made to crest nor supporters; these have remained unchanged from the time of James's accession in 1603 until the present day. It will be noticed that the *double tressure* which surrounds the Scottish lion is discontinued where the coat is joined to that of England. This is an old heraldic convention which affects all forms of border when arms are shown side by side, that is *impaled*.

This new version of the arms was short-lived as Anne died in 1714 and, under the terms of the Act of Settlement of 1701, George, Elector of Hanover, Duke of Brunswick and Luneburg and Arch Treasurer of the Holy Roman Empire, succeeded to the throne. Another reshuffle was called for in order to make reference to his German dominions. This was easily effected by removing the last quartering, which was only a repetition of the first, and substituting a coat divided into three, containing the two lions of Brunswick, the lion and hearts of Luneburg and the white horse of Hanover. The little shield in the centre, which will be seen in the illustration of this coat, has on it a representation of the crown of Charlemagne. This was the badge of office of the Arch Treasurer of the Empire; other members of the royal family never showed this shield.

In 1801 the royal arms were altered yet again in order to reflect better the new kingdom of Great Britain and Ireland created by the Act of Union with Ireland in 1800. The opportunity was taken to remove the French arms, an excision which some might think several hundred years overdue. The three kingdoms were each given a quartering, the arms of England being repeated in the last quarter in the cause of symmetry. The German arms were placed in the centre, thus enabling the Electoral Bonnet, which by right should have ensigned them, to be shown. This shield is illustrated whilst next to it is the same shield ensigned by the crown which replaced the bonnet in 1816. Under the terms of the Congress of Vienna the electorate, which had disappeared when Napoleon overthrew the Empire, was erected into a kingdom.

THE HOUSE OF SAXE-COBURG-GOTHA

1901-10

EDWARD VII 1901-10

Opposite: Four generations of the monarchy. From left to right:
Prince George, Duke of York (later George v), Queen Victoria,
Prince Edward, Duke of Windsor (later Edward viii) and Edward,
Prince of Wales (later Edward vii).

THE ROYAL ARMS

GEORGE IV AND WILLIAM IV SUCCEEDED to both the British and German possessions and so bore the post-1816 version of the arms unaltered.

On the death of William IV in 1837 the crowns were divided. That of Great Britain devolved upon his niece Victoria but that of Hanover, as it could not pass to a woman, went to the next male heir, William's brother Ernest Augustus, Duke of Cumberland.

Queen Victoria removed the shield and crown from the centre of the arms and was left with the royal arms as borne today by the present Queen. In the illustration are included three representations of the royal crown. That on the left was often used by Victoria, although it is strictly speaking incorrect; that in the centre was also used by Victoria later in her reign, whilst that on the right was used by George V and George VI.

The point to remember is that the shape of the crown is not significant, other than it reflects the artistic taste of the sovereign. What is important is that the crown in the arms is the royal crown, symbolising St Edward's crown, which is used at a coronation, itself symbolising the temporal authority and dominion of the sovereign under God.

It is sometimes remarked that now that the Queen is Queen of Canada, Australia and various other Commonwealth countries, the royal arms should symbolise this fact. Against doing this it must be argued that the constant comings and goings within the Commonwealth would necessitate endless alteration of the royal arms, which would be impracticable. The problem has been solved by there being separate arms for each of the Commonwealth kingdoms, in which the crown is the unifying factor.

The other question that is often raised is the apparent neglect of Wales, which has never featured in the royal arms. This is because Wales was never a separate kingdom, ruled by an English king. In 1302 it was absorbed into England but became a principality. Today Wales is represented armorially in the arms of the Prince of Wales. Over the royal arms he bears the old arms of the princes of North Wales, now used to represent the whole principality, ensigned by the coronet of the heir apparent.

EDWARD VII *r.* 1901-10

PRINCE ALBERT EDWARD, the future King Edward VII, was born at St James's Palace in London on 9 November 1841, the second child and eldest son of Queen Victoria and Prince Albert. The title of Prince of Wales was conferred on him when he was twenty-five days old. His father had clear ideas as to the education and training which were necessary for a future king; above all, he wished to prevent him from reverting to the pleasure-loving and immoral life of George IV and Queen Victoria's other uncles. He provided him with a number of suitable tutors, and gave them precise instructions as to how they should perform their duties. The tutors themselves considered that the regimen was too strict, and that the child was likely to go to the bad under the pressure to which he was subjected; and the constant moral exhortation was combined with a lack of parental affection, because the Queen and Prince Albert were convinced that their eldest son 'Bertie' had no intelligence or gifts of application.

It was perhaps because of this pressure and this lack of affection that the Prince of Wales, as a child, often indulged in outbursts of rage that alarmed his tutors as well as his parents. As a boy he showed a lack of consideration, and even signs of cruelty, which gave some cause for alarm. Prince Albert, although he impressed upon him that a gentleman should show consideration for the feelings of his inferiors and servants, was distressed to find that at the age of seventeen he tormented his valet by pouring wax over his new livery, water on his clean linen, and by rapping him on the nose. The Prince of Wales soon abandoned behaviour of this kind, and in later life showed a warm-hearted loyalty to his friends and consideration for his servants. His

Opposite: A king in waiting: Edward, Prince of Wales, looks particularly dashing in the astrakhan fur trim and frogging of his dragoon uniform. He was renowned for his easy manners, love of society and sense of style.

A unique photograph of the Prince of Wales, the future King Edward VII, and Queen Alexandria on their wedding day, 10 March 1863. Edward rejected six eligible German princesses before marrying Alexandria.

natural assertiveness manifested itself in such harmless ways as blaming his partner when he lost at bridge or ordering the replanning of a golf course when he did badly at the game, and sometimes in making caustic remarks about his friends' style of dress.

The Prince of Wales performed his first important public duty at the age of eighteen, when the Queen and her government agreed, with some misgivings, to send him on a state visit to Canada and the United States in 1860. The idea of sending a member of the British royal family to the United States was indeed a novelty, because the United States was generally regarded in Britain as a land of dangerous republicans and democrats. But the Prince's visit was a great success. He endeared himself to the American people by visiting George Washington's grave in Virginia, and by his charm at the balls and receptions in Washington, where it was noticed that he showed a great interest in pretty girls.

This interest involved him in an unfortunate incident soon after his return to Britain. When he was nineteen, in 1861, he was sent on manoeuvres with the army at the Curragh in Ireland. Some of his brother-officers arranged for an actress to be smuggled into his tent one night. In due course the news of the incident reached his mother and father. Prince Albert reacted violently, though he respected the Prince of Wales for his refusal to name the officers responsible. Prince Albert died a few weeks later. Queen Victoria believed that his grief at 'Bertie's' misconduct at the Curragh had shortened his life and declared that she would never be able to look at 'that boy' without a shudder.

In 1863 the Prince of Wales married Princess Alexandra of Denmark. Queen Victoria was charmed by Princess Alexandra's beauty and her respectful affection; but the marriage led to political differences between the Queen and the Prince of Wales. When Prussia and Austria went to war with Denmark in 1864 over Schleswig-Holstein, Queen Victoria's sympathies were with the German states; but the Prince of Wales supported his wife's nation, as did Palmerston and Russell, the prime minister and Foreign Secretary, and most of the British people. The Prince of Wales gave further offence to his mother in the same year by visiting Garibaldi when the Italian revolutionary general came to England, and, to the Queen's indignation, was enthusiastically welcomed in London by the people and by society alike. Queen Victoria sternly reprimanded the Prince of Wales, who defended his conduct and insisted on taking the responsibility on himself when Queen Victoria blamed his Controller, General Knollys, for having arranged the interview with Garibaldi.

For the remaining thirty-seven years of Queen Victoria's reign, the Prince of Wales played his part in public life. The Queen refused to agree to the suggestion made by several of her ministers that he should be permitted to see the state papers; nor would she accept the offers he made from time to time to visit some foreign sovereign or statesman in an attempt to help reach a settlement of an international crisis. But he increasingly performed the duties of opening bridges and public buildings, which now for the first time in history became one of the functions of the royal family. He also paid many state visits to European countries, including Russia; and in 1875-6 he spent four months in India. His chief interest, however, was the pursuit of pleasure. His life was a round of visits to large country houses, with shooting, gambling and attendance at race-meetings, followed by weeks in London with parties and banquets, and frequent visits abroad to Paris, the French Riviera and Marienbad in Bohemia. He did not indulge in heavy drinking, but ate five large meals every day, eating ten or more courses at some of them; and he smoked twelve large cigars and twenty cigarettes a day. By the time he was middle-aged he was fat: forty-eight inches round the waist.

His way of life did not please the Queen. She tried unsuccessfully to convince him that a pleasure-loving and immoral aristocracy provoked the loyal working classes into adopting Radical and democratic ideas. The Prince of Wales replied that the landed aristocracy was an essential bulwark of society, and that as long as they performed their public duties – for example, by acting as Lord Lieutenants of the counties – they should not be denied their pleasures. But the Prince's friends were not all members of the landed aristocracy; they included Jewish bankers and other businessmen – in fact, almost anyone who was rich enough to entertain on the scale which the Prince demanded at the house-parties which he attended and to provide the large quantity of game which was needed for a big shoot. His interest in people and his charm of manner led him to seek and obtain the friendship of outstanding individuals of all types and classes. He met the Labour leader, Joseph Arch, the founder of the National Agricultural Labourers' Union, and invited the working-class MP Henry Broadhurst to stay at his country house at Sandringham in Norfolk, though as Broadhurst did not possess evening dress, dinner was served to him in his private room in order to save him embarrassment. In Paris, the Prince of Wales became very friendly with General the Marquis de Gallifet, who had aroused the hatred of the French left wing by his wholesale executions during the suppres-

Edward VII enjoying one of his legendary shoots at Sandringham, his favourite home, in 1910.

sion of the Paris Commune of 1871, as well as with the Radical politician, Gambetta; and he accomplished the seemingly impossible task of persuading Gallifet and Gambetta to meet each other when they lunched with him at the Café Anglais. He loved company, and could not bear to be alone. It was said of him that he liked men better than books, and women better than either.

His love of the company of beautiful women was a great contrast to the attitude of his father, and caused both his mother and many of her subjects to fear that the future sovereign was reverting to the habits of the Regency. He was on terms of intimate friendship with a number of beautiful British and continental women – actresses like Lillie Langtry in London and Hortense Schneider in Paris, and French and English society beauties like the Princesse de Sagan, the Duchesse de Mouchy, Lady Brooke (the future Countess of Warwick) and the Hon. Mrs Keppel. He remained, however, on excellent terms with his wife, who was always faithful to him and adopted a tolerant and understanding attitude to his love affairs. He was an affectionate father. He was deeply distressed when his eldest son, Prince Albert Victor, Duke of Clarence, who was somewhat backward and had led a dissipated life, died at the age of twenty-eight. His second son was the future King George V.

On more than one occasion the Prince of Wales's friendships involved him in matrimonial disputes and other scandals, and the members of his household and of the government were sometimes obliged to take steps to prevent the scandal from becoming public and discrediting the royal family. On two occasions their efforts failed, and the Prince was obliged to give evidence in a court of law. In 1870 Sir Charles Mordaunt MP brought a divorce petition against his wife on the grounds of adultery with two friends of the Prince of Wales. Lady Mordaunt signed a confession admitting her adultery, not only with the two co-respondents, but also with the Prince of Wales. The Prince was

Lily Langtry, the actress, was perhaps the best known of Edward's many British and European mistresses.

Alexandra, wife of Edward VII, in her coronation robes with her six pages, pictured on the day of the coronation itself, 9 August 1902.

subpoenaed as a witness, but his denial of Lady Mordaunt's allegation was generally accepted, and the court held that Lady Mordaunt was insane. The evidence, however, proved that the Prince had on several occasions visited Lady Mordaunt in the afternoons when her husband was in the House of Commons and had been alone with her, which was enough to show, in the language of the time, that his conduct had been indiscreet if not improper.

Greater scandal was caused by the baccarat case twenty years later. In September 1890 the Prince of Wales stayed with a house-party at Tranby Croft in Yorkshire when he was visiting the races at Doncaster during the St Leger week. In the evenings the guests played the illegal card-game of baccarat, and one of them, Colonel Sir William Gordon-Cumming, was accused of cheating. It was agreed that the matter should be kept secret if Colonel Gordon-Cumming promised never to play cards again; but the secret leaked out, and though the Prince of Wales exerted great pressure to prevent the case from coming to court, Gordon-Cumming sued some of the other players for slander, and at the trial in July 1891 the Prince was subpoenaed as a witness. Public opinion was shocked that the Prince of Wales had played an illegal card-game, and that, although he held the rank of Field Marshal in the army, he had committed an offence under the Queen's Regulations by agreeing to suppress the fact that Gordon-Cumming had cheated, instead of reporting it to Gordon-Cumming's commanding officer. The Prince was strongly censured in the press, the *Daily Chronicle* commenting that 'his taste for the lowest type of gambling ... has profoundly shocked, we may even say disgusted, the people who may one day be asked to submit to his rule'.

The Prince was fifty-nine when Queen Victoria died in January 1901, and he ascended the throne as King Edward VII. His reign, which gave its name to a historical era, lasted only nine years. It was an age of social change and great intellectual brilliance; but the King had little sympathy with either development, though he enjoyed more serious theatre as well as musical comedies. The great Liberal triumph in the general election of 1906 led to the introduction of old age pensions, national insurance and the first steps in the creation of the modern welfare state, while the Trades Disputes Act changed trade unions from persecuted into privileged bodies. Politically, the King's sympathies were with the Conservatives; he opposed the demand for votes for women as strongly as the proposal to appoint 'natives' to the Viceroy's Council in India. But as always personalities meant more to him than politics. He was on friendly terms with his first Conservative prime minister, Lord Salisbury, but did not like Salisbury's Conservative successor, Arthur Balfour; after the Liberals came to power he liked Campbell-Bannerman, though he had strongly condemned his pro-Boer attitude during the Boer War, and was less friendly with his last Liberal prime minister, the Liberal Imperialist, Asquith. He took a more active interest in defence matters, supporting the vigorous and modern-minded naval policy of the First Sea Lord, Admiral Sir John Fisher, against the more orthodox views of the other admirals.

The fifty-nine-year-old King Edward VII's coronation procession passes through Parliament Square.

A photograph of King Edward VII with his nephew Kaiser Wilhelm II of Germany. Edward personally disliked Wilhelm, while the Kaiser was convinced that Edward had schemed to build anti-German coalitions.

It was in connection with foreign affairs that the King's influence was most marked. As he pursued the same round of pleasure in which he had engaged as Prince of Wales, he closely followed international developments, and used the occasion of his visits abroad to strengthen Britain's ties of friendship with her allies and to prevent the outbreak of a European war. His state visit to Paris in 1903 marked the beginning of the *Entente Cordiale* between Britain and France, though it would be wrong to attribute this fundamental reversal of British foreign policy either to King Edward's personal dislike of his nephew, the German

Kaiser William II, or to his popularity in Paris. He followed up the visit to Paris with state visits to Athens, Oslo, Berlin and Stockholm, and a meeting with Tsar Nicholas II on their yachts at the Russian Baltic port of Reval (Tallin) in 1908. This last meeting caused some controversy in Britain, owing to the hatred felt by socialists and Radicals for the oppressive Tsarist regime in Russia, with its pogroms of Jews and its banishment of political opponents to Siberia. King Edward's action in visiting the Tsar was criticised by three Liberal and Labour MPs in the House of Commons. The King retaliated by refusing to invite the three members to his garden-party for MPs at Buckingham Palace.

King Edward's efforts to preserve peace in Europe by personal affability won him the nickname of 'Edward the Peacemaker' in Britain, and inspired a popular music-hall song: 'There'll be no war, as long as there's a King like good King Edward.' They were viewed differently in Germany. The German Kaiser considered him to be a Machiavellian enemy who was building up anti-German coalitions. He was attacked in the German press, and after the outbreak of war in 1914 German propagandists placed the blame for it on the scheming and nefarious Edward VII.

In the last year of his life, Britain faced the greatest constitutional crisis since the Reform Bill of 1832 when the Conservative majority in the House of Lords threw out the Budget of the Liberal Chancellor of the Exchequer, Lloyd George, and the Liberal government thereupon set out to abolish the veto of the House of Lords on legislation. The government hoped to force the House of Lords to pass the Bill abolishing their veto by threatening to ask the King to create a sufficient number of new Liberal peers to give the government a majority in the House of Lords. The King was very unwilling to take this step, and worked hard to reach a compromise; he deplored both the provocative attacks on the Lords by Lloyd George and Winston Churchill and the uncompromising attitude of the 'die-hard' Tories. After another Liberal victory in the general election of January 1910, Asquith asked the King for a promise that he would create new peers if necessary; but King Edward insisted that the issue should first be put to the electorate in another general election, and meanwhile tried again to find a compromise by arranging private talks between the party leaders.

At the height of the crisis the King died, after a short illness, on 6 May 1910, at the age of sixty-eight, leaving the constitutional crisis to be solved in the reign of his son, King George V.

INDEX

PICTURE CREDITS

Christie's Images: endpapers, pages 28, 33, 39, 51, 76
theartarchive: pages 2, 13, 19, 23, 44, 57, 61, 63, 74
AKG London: pages 8, 20, 40, 43, 68-69, 73, 83
British Museum: page 14
Mary Evans Picture Library: page 15
Sotheby's Picture Library; pages 16-17
Topham Picturepoint: pages 27, 34-35, 47, 85 (top)
The Bridgeman Art Library, London: pages 37, 49, 54, 59, 62, 67, 71
Hulton Getty: pages 52, 80, 88, 96, 98
Weidenfeld & Nicolson Archives: pages 55, 97
Popperfoto: pages 65, 84, 85 (bottom), 94, 99, 100
Tate Gallery, London: page 66
Camera Press: page 93